VOTING

The Ultimate Act of Resistance

THE REAL TRUTH FROM THE VOTING RIGHTS BATTLEFIELDS

VOTING

The Ultimate Act of Resistance

RICHARD C. BELL

WORD ASSOCIATION PUBLISHERS
www.wordassociation.com
1.800.827.7903

Word Association Publishers
205 Fifth Avenue
Tarentum, Pennsylvania 15084
www.wordassociation.com
1.800.827.7903

ISBN: 978-1-63385-388-1

Library of Congress Control Number: 2020915058

Jacket design by Florence Yue • Photo by Jason Doiy • Interior by Jason Price

Publisher's Cataloging-In-Publication: Applied

DEDICATION

This book is dedicated with love to those who have made my wonderful and rewarding legal career possible - my lovely and forever encouraging wife Florence, my incredibly supportive late parents Esther and Ben and late grandparents Sam and Annie, my lawyer role model brother Alan, our very special dogs Bingo and the late Sadie, my very fine late mother-in-law and father-in-law, Taka and Frank, my very strong and courageous late cousin Arnie and late friend Russ and the most dedicated and smartest paralegals ever, Liz and the late Jazz.

A special thank you for inspiring me to write this book and pursue my passion for protecting voting rights goes out to the late Pulitzer Prize winning journalist Mary McGrory, my mentor as a college intern at the *Washington Star* and the late legendary Dr. Raymond Gavins, Professor of History, including African-American History, at Duke University and my mentor as an undergraduate at Duke.

Contents

PREFACE

Why now? At a critical moment in the age of dual challenges, a global pandemic and a racial inequality reawakening, everyone focuses on step one – protests, marches and raised consciousness. All great, but the time has come for step two – voting, the ultimate act of resistance. It turns anger into action and ideas into laws.

ACKNOWLEDGMENT

I need to acknowledge the integral role in my life of the late Dr. Raymond Gavins, iconic professor of history for 46 years at Duke University. He was my mentor when I was his student in African-American history classes at Duke. He was a gentle intellectual with bold achievements including being the first African-American to earn a Ph.D. at the University Of Virginia Graduate School Of Arts and Sciences and the first African-American History professor at Duke. He taught me about the critical role in history of the right to vote and the bloodshed and sacrifice that surrounded it especially for African-Americans throughout centuries. This kind and generous educator, author, scholar and caring advisor made such a profound impact on multiple generations of students at Duke. Dr. Gavins inspired my passion for protection of voting rights for all because, as Dr. Martin Luther King said, **"Voting is the foundation stone for political action"**.[1] Protection of voting rights for one person or one targeted group of voters affects all of us as we are reminded by the revered champion of civil rights and voting rights, the forever persistent Fannie Lou Hamer, **"Nobody is free until everybody is free"**.[2] Most of all, he taught me at an impressionable age that we must never forget to go beyond the history written by those in power at the time and always remember to also look at history from the perspective of the oppressed who did not get the opportunity to write the first version of history. Dr. Gavins' legacy lives on forever in his students, his books and his beautiful spirit of hope that was his timeless gift to the world.

He imparted in me the knowledge that voting is precious, fundamental and always worth fighting for at all costs. All policy, power and societal change derives from ordinary citizens moving elected officials to enact laws to reflect the will of the people at any given moment in history. When any citizen is denied that right to vote due to illegal, immoral or unethical barriers, the will of the people becomes the will of some of the people, not all of the people. When particular groups of people such as African-Americans and Latinos are targeted by forces of voter suppression, the will of the people becomes the will of some groups, but not all groups of people.

While it sounds so right and so basic that everyone eligible to vote (Any U.S. citizen 18 years or older with some state exceptions that still bar otherwise eligible ex-felons under particular circumstances[3]) should be allowed to vote, that is not the American experience for many eligible voters who have shown up at the polls for decades only to be turned away for unfair and seemingly politically motivated reasons.

This book will share my experiences as a pro bono voting rights attorney and voter protection advocate who has represented voters in court on Election Day to restore their right to vote and who has advised voters outside their polling places throughout the country to make sure their votes were cast and counted when unnecessary, but insidious roadblocks were placed in their way to strip away their right to vote.

In this age of the tragic killing of Mr. George Floyd at the hands of the police in Minneapolis, there is so much pent up anger and utter frustration with "the system". At this time of the Covid19 pandemic and the historic failure of the federal government to respond timely and responsibly in the public interest, people are rightfully fed up with "the system". In light of epic issues of existential importance such as economic inequality, the looming catastrophic effects of climate change and disparity of quality health care, education and housing, people are rightfully fed up with "the system".

Talk, hope and complaining to one another is not a plan nor is it a solution. Voting is a time-tested solution. Voting does move mountains, albeit slower than most would like, and is the first step toward making structural and fundamental social change. Since so many social, health care and economic issues today are literally a matter of life and death, voting is your ultimate act of resistance against the powers of the status quo to make them understand you are not going to take it from them anymore. You are not going away. The "powers that be" will either change with the times or lose their power. Change it is a coming, but not without voting, voting and more voting.

The title is literal. The call to action is real. The end result is up to you.

CHAPTER ONE

THE 2000 FLORIDA NIGHTMARE

While I was taught by my parents and grandparents from a young age that voting is a duty, an honor and mandatory, I started to see it through a different lens in November 2000.

Full disclosure, my politics are proudly progressive and I have been a registered Democrat forever. That aside, I believe voting rights should be an inherently non-partisan issue. Every American with any belief should have their right to vote protected during every election. Every voter should be allowed to vote and every vote should be counted. That was always and will always be my core belief.

Fast forward from my youthful core values of believing in the sanctity and power of voting and responsibility of every citizen to exercise her right to vote to the year 2000. I am watching TV on election night 2000 with my wife Florence and our sweet, now departed dog Sadie and we are set for a celebration of Al Gore's victory. We knew it would be a very tight race, but we were convinced Vice-President Gore would eke out a victory.

As political junkies forever (At my family dinner table growing up if you didn't know your politics and current events, you didn't belong there. Period.) we knew that Florida's electoral votes were critical to Gore's path to the win. So our trusted CBS election night coverage (Who's better than Dan Rather? Nobody. Ever. And he is still sharp as a tack with a selection of Texas expressions that are legendary.) started off so well. The Florida polls closed at 7:00 PM Eastern Time (except the Panhandle that closed at 8PM Eastern Time). By about 7:50 PM, CBS projected Al Gore the winner in Florida[4]. The two-person, one dog party was on in our apartment. I made my annual Election Day multiple calls to my mother and brother to compare our political analyses. We were unanimous in our view that Florida to Gore would seal the election when the other states' returns came in later in the evening. America did the right thing and Florence and Sadie could probably make it an early evening (I, as a totally addicted political junkie, like to stay up for concession speeches, acceptance speeches, political analysis and the returns in California and Hawaii.).

Almost like a dream sequence, things started to get surreal just a few hours later. We thought we heard it wrong when CBS at 10:00 PM withdrew its call of Florida for Al Gore[5]. We heard right and looked at each other in disbelief.

I called my mother and brother to confirm that this bizarre scenario was really unfolding and they concurred. What did this mean? Why was this happening? What in the world is going on in Florida?

You could feel the uncertainty in the voices of the on-air broadcasters as we started channel surfing. There was palpable turmoil. The tone, the delivery, the flurry of speculation from talking heads was unsettling. How could this be? Why would the networks call the most pivotal state for Gore so early (less than one hour after the vast majority of Florida polls closed) then take it back? Conspiracy theories swirled in our minds especially with the knowledge that George Bush's brother Jeb was the sitting Governor of Florida.

A few deep breaths and many, many snacks later, we calmed down enough to rationalize this was not a state called for Bush, it was just back in the "too close to call" category but would certainly go back to Gore when the networks confirmed their earlier data. Yes, a bit nerve-wracking. No, not a game changer. Certainly not anything more than an over-cautious call by the networks for now. Of course they would later project Gore the winner of Florida and our next President as winner of the Electoral College. Oh, Florida. If only.

10:00 PM turned into 11:00 PM, then midnight and no new CBS call on Florida. Still "too close to call". By 2:17AM, the political world in my household (and many, many others) came crashing down with a thud heard 'round the world.[6]

CBS reversed its two earlier projections (For Gore, then "too close to call") and called Florida for Bush thereby projecting George W. Bush as the President-Elect.

What? Can't be. Unprecedented. Not real. Must be a nightmare. Flipping around the channels, we realized it was the way virtually every network was going. Horrifying. Soul crushing. Bone chilling. Looking at Dan Rather, all I could say to my TV was, "Gore won, now you said Bush won. Come on Dan. Help me out here Dan. You never failed me before tonight".

Well, Florence and Sadie shared my depressed and exasperated state and went to bed after Dan announced the CBS projection for Bush in the wee hours of the morning. I could just not accept that was true especially with the thought in my head that there were shenanigans going on in the Sunshine State. It just sounded wrong, fishy and suspicious that it was on the watch of Bush's brother Jeb whose team oversaw the machinery – literally and figuratively – of Florida elections.

I said telephone goodnights to my mother and brother and told Florence and Sadie I will be up all night because something is not right and our democracy is in peril and needs me on watch. This election just smells and I cannot believe it's over. So I just continued to watch Dan Rather and all the political commentary and election projection data explanations going on and on. I still held out hope.

My wife's friend from the west coast was also in a furor and funk and called our land line after the 2:17 AM Bush projection as did Florence's mother from San Francisco. I was now holding two phones simultaneously as commiserator-in-chief at 3:45 in the morning. Florence's friend was ranting, raving and commiserating, but I told her Florence was sound asleep and I couldn't wake her because there was no change in the news and Gore was expected to make a formal concession speech. He had allegedly made a private congratulatory call to George Bush earlier.

Then at 3:57 AM in the east, lightning struck from the heavens[7]. Dan Rather, who in my sleep-deprived state I believed was addressing me personally, told the world that Bush was no longer the projected President-Elect, CBS was withdrawing its Florida projection and the race in Florida was once again "too close to call". Florence's friend and I screamed with joy on the phone. I told her I need to hang up and tell Florence and I burst open the bedroom door about 4:00AM and like a madman screamed "Bush didn't win. No one won yet. Florida is too close to call." Florence and Sadie jumped up out of their beds and looked at me like I was hallucinating. I just kept screaming and told them to come in the living room and listen to Dan. Sure enough, Dan and most of the other networks rescinded the call for Bush and we knew it was game on for a Florida win or a recount. What we didn't know was that voting in America would never be the same.

The morning hours turned into afternoon then evening and no winner was declared again in Florida. The hours turned into days, the days turned into weeks and the court-house turned into the arena where the election might be decided as the folly of the hanging chads Florida recount began in earnest.

My obsession with a fair and just recount became more so by the day. The world of vote counting, lawsuit electoral challenges and political/media spin was on steroids. My level of frustration and helplessness became a fervor as I furiously tried to figure out how I could help the obvious confusion, incompetence and potential chicanery going on during the Florida recount.

As the weeks went on, I got an email sent to me by a lawyer friend which was seeking out-of-state lawyers to come to Florida to assist the Gore team as "observers" of the Florida recount. I WAS ECSTATIC. I found my calling and it was a phone call away from happening.

When the organization in charge of the Democratic recount observers got back to me, I felt so exhilarated and finally useful in the American drama of "The Florida Recount – Day 16, 26, 29 . . .". I literally had an assignment while there was a pending ruling from the Florida Supreme Court on whether a statewide manual recount would be ordered. On December 8th by a 4-3 vote the Florida Supreme Court ordered an immediate manual recount of all ballots in the state where no vote for President was machine-recorded which was estimated to be 45,000 ballots.[8] Oh yes. Let the games begin.

My assignment was in South Florida (the specific precinct was not yet determined) and I was in the process of making airplane and hotel reservations when that fateful day of December 9th arrived. Within 24 hours of the Florida Supreme Court decision ordering the recount, the U.S. Supreme Court dashed all of my hopes and dreams of participating in the defense of free and fair elections in Florida. By a 5-4 decision, the U.S. Supreme Court halted the manual recount that had resumed again in Florida.[9] I felt the same shock and emptiness that I had on election night when the news went from Gore winning Florida to "too close to call" to Bush winning Florida to "too close to call". It was a devastating replay of that awful evening just a month earlier.

I had a sick feeling once the Supreme Court got involved in the recount since most legal commentators opined that the Florida election was a state issue that the Supreme Court would punt on as to not appear partisan. Time was not kind to that projection.

No need for airplane or hotel reservations. It was back to being a spectator awaiting the U.S. Supreme Court's oral arguments and its final decision in Bush v. Gore. After the stay of the recount (5-4), I was not feeling good about where this election recount was going. All of my reading of Supreme Court decisions in law school and in my law practice was done with a reverence for the intellect of the court. Now I was feeling politics replaced intellect on this conservative court. I held out hope, but the inspiring decision by the Florida

Supreme Court to settle the election at the ballot box with a systematic and transparent manual recount was fading like the final puff of a sunset.

So the recount was up against a date of December 12th to finish (the "safe harbor" date by which the Florida "electors" needed to be chosen for the December 18th Electoral College convention) and the Supreme Court stayed the recount until hearing oral arguments and finally deciding on December 12th. What? How can that make sense? The court believes the last date to finish the recount is December 12th and they halt the recount on December 9th, hear oral argument on December 11th and decide the case on December 12th? Is that any way to hold free and fair elections in America? I just could not believe this was happening.

Well, of course it really was happening. On December 12th at about 10:00 PM, the court issued an opinion which, in essence, decided that the recount process ordered by the Florida Supreme Court was flawed but instead of ordering a recount that fixed the "flaw" the majority determined time had run out for a recount which effectively said Bush wins Florida and the presidency.[10] As Justice Breyer's dissent powerfully explained in plain language "The Court was wrong to take this case. It was wrong to grant a stay. It should now vacate the stay and permit the Florida Supreme Court to decide whether the recount should resume. The political implications of this case for the country are momentous".[11]

As a lawyer who believes in fairness, justice and equality, I was completely devastated. I had always had the highest reverence for the integrity of the Supreme Court and that day forever changed my view of it from a venerable legal institution to a brazenly political institution. I felt like the law was trashed and the election was decided by 5 justices in Washington instead of the millions of voters in Florida. It was a crushing blow to my respect for the Supreme Court. The majority opinion read as intellectually dishonest.

There have been horrible decisions of the court in generations past especially regarding segregation and the rights of African-Americans. I naively thought the court by the year 2000 had moved on from that unforgivable denial of fairness and justice. Bush v. Gore told me that naked political favoritism trumped all. How awful. How ugly. How un-American.

As distressing as it was, in a short time I knew I needed to attack the problem with a solution, not wallow in the wrong perpetrated by the court.

The rest of this book follows that journey.

CHAPTER TWO

"Son, I grew up in Mississippi"

After the sickening disappointment of 2000, I knew I needed to get involved in the next Presidential election in an effective way. The roles played by the Governor and Secretary of State of Florida, coupled with the U.S. Supreme Court's legally flawed and obviously partisan decision, left me motivated to find my own role in protecting voting rights.

Having been denied my opportunity to be a recount observer by the U.S. Supreme Court's halting of the manual Florida recount, I thought back to a moment in either the late 90's or early 2000's that I experienced in an airport in Southeast Asia when coming back from a vacation. I was standing in line when I spotted a man nearby with a jacket that identified him as an "international election observer". I went over to him to inquire about the words on the jacket. He told me that he was travelling back from observing a recent election in Southeast Asia as part of an international team of observers monitoring the voting process for fairness and integrity. How fascinating and important I thought to myself. It planted a seed in my head as to what I should be doing one day. Sadly, the need would be in the United States, not a troubled developing country. We were clearly a troubled country with a flawed voting system and the time had come to play my small role in fixing that process.

While I had volunteered for many campaigns over the years since my youth doing canvassing and phone calls, I now realized my training as a trial attorney afforded me special skills in the fight for free and fair elections. The time was now to formally enter the battle for voting rights. I was ready and the country was in obvious need of election protection attorneys.

In 2004 as a John Kerry supporter, I contacted the campaign and found out that there was an entire division of the volunteer base dedicated to recruiting election protection attorneys and concerned citizens. The effort was organized, strong and ready. All it needed was willing volunteers.

I wanted to go to a swing state and a city that was a bastion of expected voter suppression. All signs pointed to Cleveland, Ohio. Since Ohio was expected to decide the Electoral College, a strong turnout for Kerry in Cleveland was an absolute necessity to counter the Bush strongholds in other parts of the state. Also, since 2000 it seemed that reports of voter suppression were on the rise and the overwhelming targets were African-Americans and Latino voters.

Cleveland has a high percentage of African-American voters and any attempts at suppressing their votes, subtly or directly, was alleged in the public square to be a possible strategy to keep the Cleveland vote total down.

With pent up excitement from my almost voter protection role in Florida in 2000, I signed up to fight the good fight in Cleveland for Election Day 2004. As with all volunteer campaign efforts, the expenses of flights, hotel and meals were borne by me. I also had to take a number of days out of my law practice in New York City since I left on the Friday before Election Day with plans to return on the Wednesday night thereafter. It was a true no-brainer since I was finally going to do something that could make a real difference in defending the right to vote in America where it was most needed.

Before the campaign accepted me, I was required to pass a short test on Ohio voting laws after studying those laws that were provided to me by the campaign. While I was not, of course, appearing in court in Ohio or giving Ohio legal advice (I have never, of course, given out-of-state legal advice in any campaign) my job was to stand outside a polling place and ensure that voters understood the procedures to follow and to direct them to the proper authorities if they were denied the right to vote.

I took my role very seriously since my former history professor, Dr. Raymond Gavins, always stressed how the right to vote was a foundational action in enacting and preserving civil rights in America especially for African-Americans whose struggle for equality was a continuum still progressing quite slowly after almost 400 years. As I drove to my hotel in downtown Cleveland, I felt like a boxer doing the ring walk before the championship fight. I was so ready to get this righteous fight started.

Armed with all my knowledge of Ohio voting laws, I couldn't wait to use my information. The parking valet at the hotel, a nice young man, took my keys and asked why I was in town. As I was telling him, I asked, "Are you registered to vote?". He proudly said "Of course." I then inquired about his friends and relatives. When he said he believed so, I gave him a phone number for all of them to call to check on their registration status and to confirm the location of their polling places. He was very receptive to my suggestion and wrote it down. He even asked me some questions for his friends and relatives about potential voting issues (address changes, DMV changes, etc.) as the days went on. I really felt useful. He had no idea how good he made me feel that I came to Cleveland to ensure everyone who wanted to vote did vote and every vote got counted.

On Saturday, I showed up at Kerry headquarters to get my assignment. I told them I wanted to go to an area where voter suppression was expected and a place that most

14

out-of-state white lawyers might not sign up for because it was in an economically depressed area with a high concentration of African-American voters (Let's be real. Most white lawyers do not spend their days or nights in these neighborhoods. Sadly, lots of defacto segregation exists in both the work world and the social world. Sad, but true.). I knew that those were target areas for forces that wanted to keep the Democratic and African-American vote down.

I got an ideal assignment. It was a polling place inside a public housing project. The project and the surrounding area were heavily African–American and there were suspicions that "challengers" from the Republican Party would be challenging voters inside the polls based on a variety of specious allegations (signature matches, address changes, etc.). Just the word voter poll place "challengers" sounded absurd to me since I believe that anyone who meets the basic requirements (U.S. Citizen, 18 years old or older and resident of the county and state) should always be allowed to vote with no hyper-technical legal barriers. Voting in the world's oldest continuing democracy should be easy, not hard, right?[12]

I would not be inside the polls since only Ohio residents were permitted to do that task. They were allowed to observe the voting process inside and report to me to inform headquarters if any challenges or pattern of challenges seemed to violate Ohio election procedures.

My job would be to stand outside (more than 100 feet from the polling place) to assist voters with any voting questions or problems they may have on the way in or out of the polling place. Those questions ranged from whether their registration was valid (I had a phone number to call to verify that), whether they were in the right location (same phone number) and whether anyone attempted to intimidate, obstruct or confuse them while attempting to exercise their right to vote (those would be reported by me to headquarters for investigation and resolution).

Essentially, the outside poll observer is the eyes and ears of the campaign to assist individual voters with voting issues, discern if any nefarious patterns of voter intimidation/obstruction are happening and ensure that there are not unusually long lines developing that require resolution by local election authorities or the courts. Long lines mean frustrated, impatient voters who may give up and not vote. Long lines in certain communities always seem like a voter suppression tactic since they anecdotally always seem to pop up in African-American neighborhoods.

Before Election Day, however, I was assigned to do canvassing in different Cleveland area locations to pass out leaflets about polling places, voting procedures and to answer voter questions leading up to the Tuesday voting day. My first day, Saturday, I was assigned to go with a random partner. He was a very nice gentleman who seemed to be recognized by a number of people at campaign headquarters. We went together covering a neighborhood by criss-crossing the houses on the block. He did look familiar, but I couldn't picture him.

Having done canvassing in the past, I knew the response rate would be minimal, but every positive encounter was a chance to pass on valuable voting information to a potential voter. At the very least, every door got an informational pamphlet listing valuable information about registration information, poll information and key phone numbers and websites.

At the end of the day, I finally asked my partner why so many people at headquarters had recognized him. It turned out he was quite a famous actor who had been married to another famous actress (I will keep his identity anonymous because he sought no special treatment and never would have identified himself if I didn't ask.). He was so humble and self-effacing. He had flown in from Los Angeles because he too needed to stand up for free and fair elections especially at a time when such issues as the war in Iraq, domestic security balanced with civil rights and court appointments were paramount in America. I was very proud to stand with him to help our democracy in a meaningful way.

I continued to do the canvassing through the Monday before Election Day. There were rumors circulating that flyers were being placed on cars in African-American neighborhoods in metropolitan Cleveland that contained such misinformation that Democrats were to vote on different days and polling place locations had changed. Such evil, anti-American behavior made me furious. I was sure to dispel these rumors when residents answered my door knocks throughout the weekend.

Then on Sunday everything changed for me as I approached a particular house in a predominantly African-American suburb adjacent to Cleveland. I walked up a pathway to a house armed with my flyers, tons of voter information ready to repeat to anyone who would listen and my directive that I and other voter protection attorneys would be outside polling places to assist with any problems, complaints or issues related to potential voter suppression. I rarely found a person at home (or willing to answer the door in an area flooded with volunteers for days due to the importance of Cleveland as the potential producer of the deciding votes for an Electoral College win for Kerry in Ohio, the battleground of all battlegrounds in 2004).

I rang the bell at this nice-looking house and the door opened slowly to reveal an elderly African-American woman who later told me she was in her 90's. She was soft spoken but had a very firm and determined voice. She listened respectfully to my informational "speech", but when I got to the part about being a voter protection attorney on Election Day, she politely stopped me and said words that have stayed with me for the past 16 years. She said, "Son, I grew up in Mississippi of the 30's, 40's, 50's and 60's. I know a lot about barriers to voting. No one will ever again take away my right to vote. Don't you worry about me. Just help others who haven't seen what I've seen."

Profound. Deep. Raw. Her words were delivered with such quiet passion from the depths of her experiences. I thanked her for her wisdom and promised her I would do everything in my power to "help others". I have thought back to that woman's words every time I have done voter protection work in the past 16 years. I made her a promise that I must forever keep. Her words embody everything about the sacrifice made by so many in generations past to protect and honor the right to vote. I read about the sanctity of the right to vote in many history books and articles. All of those were important. None brought it to life quite like that woman who obviously fought the battle in Jim Crow Mississippi on the front lines. She is the true warrior. She is the true hero. She is my inspiration every Election Day. We must never forget her words because any voter denied is really every voter denied.

Of course, my motivation to do my job well on Election Day 2004 was figuratively on steroids after that fateful encounter. I went to my polling place at the public housing project the day before Election Day to introduce myself to the property manager and staff so they wouldn't see some stranger arrive from nowhere at the premises. When I arrived on Monday morning, I think they were a bit surprised but were very welcoming. I explained that I would be outside the whole time so they told me where I could use their bathroom facilities if necessary on Election Day. They even offered me a cup of coffee and introduced me to some residents who said they often congregate in the lobby early so be sure to say hello on Tuesday. I obviously lucked out with a nice assignment.

I arrived Tuesday at about 5:00 AM (An hour and a half early to make sure I was prompt) on a day that turned out to be on and off rain. I saw there were some people in the lobby so I went inside to say hello and re-introduce myself. They told me the polls wouldn't be set up for a while so they invited me to sit with them and have some coffee and pastries. What a delightful way to start the day.

The next 13 hours that the polling place was open consisted of me yelling in the on again, off again rain to any voter in ear shot that I was there to help with any voting questions or issues. My voter protection partner was inside the polls (a Cleveland resident allowed inside by law) to make sure the Republican "challenger" played by the rules. I had two lovely people outside with me who were handing out flyers relating to local elections. They got a real kick out of my incessant yelling out to voters even when the rain got heavy. We had a lot of laughs and they were so kind as to bring me sandwiches, snacks and water throughout the day. Paula, a very kind and civic-minded advocate, has remained in touch with me to this day. She is very dedicated to local causes and issues and is a model for citizen activists. Also, she was very kind and generous to this stranger on a long, rainy day in Cleveland out of the goodness of her heart.

The actual issues at my polling place were minimal. Most of the problems related to people being at the wrong polling place which I easily resolved with a phone call. Long lines, broken machines and obvious acts of voter suppression never materialized in my precinct. I spoke with hundreds of voters outside that day and they genuinely seemed to be pleased that there was a voter protection volunteer outside the polls to answer their questions and head off any shenanigans before they began.

One poignant moment did arise later in the day. There was an important local education funding issue on the ballot in my district. An elderly African-American man was walking near me as I called out that my role was to help voters. He told me he was illiterate, but he wanted to vote on the school funding issue "to help the kids". He said he did not really read and wouldn't know how to cast a ballot. I told him he was entitled to voter assistance inside and all he had to do was ask the poll workers. I advised him he had an absolute right to that assistance and should not leave until he got it and cast his ballot as he wished.

It was quite a long while before he came out that evening. I was concerned he was having a problem. He finally came out and with a tear in his eye he said "I voted to help the kids. A lady inside helped me fill out the ballot". I also had a tear in my eye as I congratulated him for exercising his right to vote and told him the kids would be very thankful for his vote. Later in the evening, my voter protection partner inside confirmed for me that all went well for him. He told the people inside what I had told him and he got the voting assistance that he was entitled to by law. That's the America I love. The one that ensures voting for everyone who is a citizen and 18 or over regardless of a disability such as illiteracy. What a wonderful result for a kind-hearted man who could not read but wanted to make sure the local schools were fully funded so all children could be taught to read to avoid his unfortunate fate.

Why is voting the ultimate act of resistance? Ask that defiant woman from Mississippi and that man who voted "to help the kids". They resisted the barriers of voter suppression and illiteracy to exercise their right to vote and support candidates and issues important to them. They resisted those that oppose voting laws that make it as easy and seamless as possible to vote and create positive change through the political process.

At the end of an exhausting day after standing outside for 13 hours, I headed back to my hotel excited to watch better election night returns than in 2000. As the night drew late, my hunch (go to Cleveland) was right and the Electoral College victory came down to the swing state of Ohio. There was no clear winner as the night went on and CNN had not even made a projection by early Wednesday afternoon.[13] During the early morning hours, Vice Presidential candidate John Edwards promised that the campaign would "fight for every vote" and showed no sign of conceding Ohio.[14]

There were allegations of voter irregularities in Ohio during Election Day so that promoted a narrative that Ohio would be contested if Bush were declared the winner. I woke up early Wednesday determined to extend my stay in

Cleveland as a recount observer or in another role if a recount were necessary. I went to a local Kerry headquarters to offer my services and was told everything was in flux and to check back later. I decided to catch lunch at a local diner nearby that had a TV on where I could watch the developing election news. Was this going to be 2000 all over again?

I had hope based on John Edwards' earlier statement about counting every vote, but my heart got broken soon after I sat down in the diner. Kerry was about to concede without a fight. Concede the razor thin margin in Ohio with reported voting irregularities throughout the state? Please let that not be the case. I watched with great disappointment as Kerry gave up before my eyes on TV. As I kept shaking my head and muttering out loud, I caught the attention of an older woman who was alone in the booth facing me. We started to commiserate and I finally told her I'm coming over to her booth to continue our shared frustration together.

The conversation with my new friend Monica was the beginning of a beautiful friendship. My wife and I have visited her in Cleveland a number of times over the past 16 years and she has stayed with us back east. She has become a very dear friend. Despite another crushing Election Day result, 2004 will always leave me with a gift of meeting Monica, a wonderful friend and beautiful human being. Or as she signs all her many cards to us "Love, Your Cleveland Friend Monica". She also taught me never to say "goodbye", but rather "so long". It's a much more hopeful way to end a conversation.

As I flew home later on Wednesday, with sadness over the election results (and Kerry's failure to contest Ohio), I thought about that defiant woman from Mississippi, that gentleman who triumphed over illiteracy to vote to "help the kids" and the lovely people and voters I met in Cleveland. Overall, it was a very impactful learning experience that left me with exhilaration and hope. I got to make a difference for a number of voters and for that I am very grateful. The taste of voter protection just made me hungry for more. And more I got since voter suppression is tragically a continuing way of life in America.

Kerry's failure to contest the election in Ohio looks even worse in retrospect. In 2005, the U.S. House of Representatives, House Judiciary Committee Democratic Staff issued a comprehensive report after it investigated alleged irregularities in the Ohio vote for President.[15] The report concluded that "We have found numerous, serious election irregularities in the Ohio Presidential election, which resulted in a significant disenfranchisement of voters. Cumulatively, these irregularities, which affected hundreds of thousands of votes and voters in Ohio, raise grave doubts regarding whether it can be said the Ohio electors select-ed on December 13, 2004, were chosen in a manner that conforms to Ohio law, let alone federal requirements and constitutional standards."[16]

While my particular polling place in Cleveland ran smoothly, the same cannot be said about the rest of Ohio according to the report[17]. Alleged errors occurred from mis-allocation of voting machines that created inordinately long lines in predominately minority and Democratic areas to intimidation by partisan "challengers" questioning voters' right to vote in the polling place to 93,000 spoiled ballots (no vote allegedly cast for president) to 10,000 official registration errors causing voters to lose their right to vote in Cuyahoga County (where Cleveland is located).[18]

Bush won Ohio by 50.81% to 48.7% or by a margin of 118,001 out of 5,600,935 votes counted.[19] That means that if a high enough percentage of the hundreds of thousands of votes questioned by the report had gone to Kerry, we would have inaugurated President Kerry in January 2005 clearly changing the course of history (Hurricane Katrina response, Iraq War handling, 2 Supreme Court appointments, etc.).

While no one can definitively conclude whether the Ohio vote would have changed if Kerry requested a recount or made other court challenges, it is fair to say that such a contest would have flushed out the facts in real time whether the alleged irregularities in Ohio amounted to significant interference with a free and fair election.

Voting rights have been a significant issue since our country's founding. It took many generations for African-Americans and women to even get the legal right to vote which doesn't always mean the actual right to vote.[20] Jim Crow laws well into the 20th century were used overtly and covertly to deny African-Americans the right to cast their ballots and have them counted.[21] The Voting Rights Act of 1965 was an act of Congress that was finally passed after decades of bloodshed in the name of equal voting rights for all.[22] The law was an excellent start. The actual experiences over centuries are another story with many ugly turns.

So now the country was left with two presidential elections in a row with at best unintentionally questionable results and at worst intentionally unfair results. Either way, the voting system was clearly broken, the disproportionate impact on minority voters and Democratic precincts was obvious and we as a country were perceived as incapable of running elections without the appearance of impropriety.

There was some effort made at reform in 2002 – the Help America Vote Act passed by Congress.[23] It was relatively tepid in its appropriation of federal funds to states to update voting equipment, establishing an Election Assistance Commission and requiring certain ID for first time registrants.[24] None of these "reforms" attacked the problems that resulted in Ohio's myriad of problems. It was clear to me and many others that there was now an overt and covert electoral strategy that targeted minority voters in a way not seen since the Jim Crow era. It was not an "official" strategy but it was surely more than a coincidence as evidenced by the presence of Republican "challengers" at targeted polls, extraordinarily long lines in predominately African-American areas, failed equipment in so many minority voting districts and registration errors in predominantly African-American areas.[25]

Florida was the fool me once, shame on you moment. Ohio was the fool me twice, shame on me moment. I now knew more than ever that I needed to continue to do my part to protect voting rights after my voter protection stint in Cleveland.

CHAPTER THREE

LET'S TAKE THIS FIGHT TO COURT

In looking for a way forward to make a real difference in the fight for voting rights, in 2005 I contacted the New York Democratic Lawyers Council. It was an esteemed organization dedicated to the protection of voting rights. I proudly joined in 2005 and was able to get onto the Minority Voting Rights Committee. I knew that's where the real action was in the field of voting rights.

The committee meetings and lectures by prominent politicians and voting experts were excellent. I learned so much about voting rights beyond my on-ground experience in Ohio. It led me to devour articles, case law and studies related to voting rights. Voting rights is a fascinating intersection of the law, politics and sociology. Fascinating, but often shockingly ugly.

As the year progressed, I looked forward to doing voter protection in New York on Election Day. Since it was an off-year for federal elections, I would not be traveling out-of-state to defend voting rights in 2005.

Then another tragedy struck America and once again there was a disproportionate negative effect on predominantly African-American communities. It was named Hurricane Katrina and its devastation in late 2005 was breathtaking. The city of New Orleans and its surrounding areas were not only crushed by the harrowing storm, but they were in so many ways abandoned by the federal government in time of need. The Bush administration response is well known as a primer on how not to handle a disaster.

It was stunning and heart-breaking to watch on television as so many predominantly poor African-American souls were begging for their lives on rooftops or trapped in their homes that were filling up with lethal amounts of water. It reminded me again of how equality and fairness are hollow words when government failures have such disparate impact on one community over another.

I thought the least I could do beyond donations was to contact people in power who could hopefully exert some immediate influence. On September 2, 2005 I sent faxes (email was not as prevalent in my personal world in 2005) to most members of the Congressional Black Caucus as well as my own congressperson and senators. This is what I wrote:

Re: Racial Genocide in New Orleans

While I am not your constituent, I believe that you are the best hope to immediately exert pressure on the federal government to bring an end to what appears from the outside like a racial genocide taking place in New Orleans because I know you care about what happens to the desperate people left in New Orleans.

Please do everything humanly possible immediately to spare the lives of those helpless victims who have suffered from three tragedies - the wrath of a terrible storm; the complete failure of the federal government to give immediate humanitarian and public safety assistance to the afflicted; and the complete failure of the federal government to prevent the engineering/urban planning disaster that it was on notice of for years according to various media reports.

Right now, your immediate public outcry for Federal humanitarian and public safety assistance and your use of your political power as a member of Congress are needed instantly.

If your actions save one life, ease one person's agony or make one sister, aunt, mother, brother or spouse an ounce more comfortable, your efforts will be heroic.

31

When all are brought to safety and accounted for in New Orleans, we can begin to sort out how the utter failure of our federal government led to the deaths and suffering of countless thousands of our fellow human beings.

Earlier, I used the very harsh term "racial genocide." The mind set of the White House before and during this disaster will probably never be revealed while this administration is in power. The results, however, of the President's inaction, both in preparation for and during the most urgent rescue phase of this tragedy, have clearly produced what looks like the aftermath of a racial genocide. Just look at the racial make-up of those left in New Orleans this week. We do not need sociologists to tell us that African-Americans are the vast majority of those failed by the federal government. We can all only speculate how the preparation and rescue would have been handled if those affected were white suburbanites in a nice middle-class setting. Enough said.

In 2004, I volunteered my time and money to help monitor the presidential election in Cleveland, Ohio. At present, I volunteer my time as an attorney with the New York City branch of the Democratic National Committee National Lawyer's Council regarding protection of voting rights with a specific committee assignment to the Minority Voting Rights Committee. My disgust with our electoral injustices has now been exceeded by my disgust with the horrors of government incompetence, indifference and paralysis when it came time to save the lives of a community that "coincidentally" is a sea of brown faces on our TV screens.

Shame on Mr. Bush! Shame on our federal government! Shame on every American who does not express outrage to our supposed leaders every single day until this racial genocide finally ends.

I happen to be a white male who has had wonderful opportunities in this great nation. It is incumbent upon all of us from every background that make up our rainbow of a country to proclaim loudly, publicly and often that there is one race on this earth that we all belong to - the human race.

Now, if we can just get those in power to remember this before the next tragedy strikes!

Thank you for your time and effort to end the death and suffering of those precious souls still clinging to life in New Orleans.

If you have any suggestions on how I can help you, please contact me as indicated below.

KEEP THE PRESSURE ON! LIVES DEPEND ON YOU!

Sincerely,
Richard C. Bell, Esq.

I wish I could tell you I got an immediate response from many of these elected officials. I did not. It does not mean that they weren't doing everything in their power to resolve the problem on the ground. It just meant that their staffs were not responding quickly to letters by people like me who were not constituents. That's fine as long as they were doing some good which seemed to be the case from news reports.

The only response I recall receiving to any of my faxes was from one of my senators and that response came months later. At least I felt like I was doing something for communities like the one I worked in during the elections in Cleveland.

The harm done to poor and African-American residents of Louisiana by the pathetic federal response to Katrina is well documented. I bring this incident up because it relates directly to the importance of our vote as the ultimate act of resistance. I find it hard to believe that a Kerry administration would have treated the residents of greater New Orleans the same way they were treated by the Bush administration. Voting has consequences. Free and fair elections allow the will of the people to rule. When voting rights are compromised or are perceived to be compromised like in Florida in 2000 and Ohio in 2004, there can be grave consequences for real people. Hurricane Katrina and its aftereffects made me think back to 2000 and 2004. Every election really is a matter of life and death for some real person. It is a matter of life or death for real people in their economic lives, their health care lives, their environmental lives regarding clean water, clean air and climate change. Resistance comes in many forms. Sometimes it manifests in a massive protest march. Sometimes it manifests in thousands of petitions sent to politicians. In the end, the goal is to reform, change and create a better path to equality for all in every sector of life. That path is built by policy, laws and implementation of both. Fundamental change gets pushed, enacted and put into practice by elected government officials from the local school board member to the mayor to the state legislature to the congressperson to the president. They all get there the same way - by winning the most votes. When the integrity of the voting system is compromised, the very foundation of the system is shattered. That is why I became convinced that protection of voting rights is protection of democracy and is protection of the right of the people to make fundamental and structural change in society. That is the ultimate act of resistance in a civil nation. That is the lesson I took away from these events of 2000, 2004 and 2005.

After the Hurricane Katrina debacle, I was more convinced than ever that my participation in voter protection could make a real difference in the lives of others. I was excited to have a different role in New York than I had in Ohio. I was going to actually be inside the polling place this time to monitor any issues that the voters had regarding challenges to registration or other issues.

A few weeks before my assignment, I was asked where in New York City my polling place was so that an assignment could be made with my location in mind. I never thought about that and was never asked that question before by the voting rights organization. Since I worked in but did not live in New York City and was obviously not a registered voter there, I was not eligible to be inside a New York City polling place as an observer. I was so disappointed but resigned myself to working outside the polls in the city.

Out of nowhere, about a week before the election a Democratic Party organization in the county where I resided in New Jersey somehow found me and asked if I would like to argue voting rights cases in court in New Jersey on Election Day since I was a licensed attorney in New Jersey as well as New York. Now that sounded very exciting.

The voter protection program in Bergen County, New Jersey was very robust. I was handed a large notebook by the organization with New Jersey election law guidelines, statutory laws, case law and practical information. There was a comprehensive preparation meeting where very experienced voting rights attorneys answered all of my questions.

As luck would have it, New Jersey is a very evolved state in the world of voting rights. After doing it now for almost eight years, I would call it a model for how states should handle voting rights issues on Election Day.

The system in New Jersey is outstanding. If a voter goes to her polling place on Election Day and is told by a poll worker that due to some registration issue that she will not be allowed to vote, she is given a written notice that she can report to the county courthouse and have an immediate hearing before a judge of the Superior Court (the trial level court in New Jersey) to determine if she will be allowed to vote under court order. The system is set up for an attorney from the New Jersey Attorney General's Office to argue the position of the polling place (i.e. usually trying to deny her the right to vote due to a variety of administrative reasons), an attorney from the New Jersey Public Advocate's office who is often present to argue on behalf of the voter and lawyers from the Democratic Party and Republican Party are who present arguments for or against the voter as well (Guess which party argues against voting?). The courthouse, closed to all other business on Election Day, is open with a sufficient number of judges and court personnel to conduct these Election Day hearings due to the importance of protecting the right to vote in real time on Election Day. If the vote is not cast on Election Day, it is almost unheard of that court intervention after the polls close will be of any practical effect for the voter who was wrongly shut out of voting on the only day that counted.

As a trial attorney, I was very used to hearings for decades so I was definitely in my element. I became thoroughly familiar with the applicable law and I was very proud to volunteer my time on Election Day to make sure every voter casts their ballot and every vote is counted. I enthusiastically signed up for both the morning and afternoon shift which meant 6:00 AM to 8:00 PM.

As the voters trickled into the courtroom, my role was to advise them that I represent the county Democratic organization but I had no interest in whether they were voting Democratic, Republican, Independent or other. I would take the voter's position to restore their right to vote. I would never ask them who they supported because our only organizational goal was to get every legally entitled voter to vote and have their vote cast and counted.

I will discuss the specifics of the hearings shortly, but a few early observations I made in court that day. Although Bergen County is in suburban New Jersey with a largely white population, the overwhelming majority of voters at the hearings to restore their right to vote were African-American and some Latinos. As we say in the law, "disparate impact" on one group of people even though it may be unintentional, is discriminatory nonetheless. For instance, Title VII of the Civil Rights Act of 1964 outlawed intentional discrimination based on race, sex and other such grounds.[26] By 1991 that law was amended to outlaw disparate impact (as well as intentional) discrimination even when there is no proof of intent by the employer to discriminate by race, sex or other protected class of individuals.[27]

I categorically do not allege that anyone intentionally discriminated against one group of people in denying their right to vote in my voter protection experience. I can with certainty communicate my observations from being on the ground in real time as to whose voting rights were actually affected. Whether it was a city like Cleveland where the African-American population was the majority group with close to 50% or Bergen County New Jersey where it was less than 10%, it seemed more than coincidental to me that the voters having issues predominately belonged to a group that had to literally fight with their lives for centuries to obtain and protect their right to vote.[28] The picture of what was really going on in the voting rights struggle became crystal clear to me the more involved I got in the world of voter protection.

As I approached the voters in the courtroom in New Jersey, I would ask them a number of questions as to their registration process, the circumstances under which they were being denied the right to vote at the polling place and other questions relating to potential legal arguments I could make on their behalf. There were a number of cases wherein voters simply moved from one county to another before the close date to register to vote. Under New Jersey law, that voter was obligated to re-register in the new county before the close of registration (29 days before the election) or forfeit the right to vote in the election. Unfair. Unjust. Archaic. These were the best arguments for same day registration on Election Day, but it wasn't the law in New Jersey at that time. Those voters were unfortunately ordered not eligible to vote in the 2005 election, but the judge always directed them to go back to the Board of Elections (across the street) after the hearing where they were processed and filled out the proper registration forms so they could vote in the next election. Very frustrating cases to lose but that was the state of the law.

Then there were a number of voters who testified under oath that they filled out registration forms at tables in front of supermarkets or at shopping malls yet their names didn't appear in the polling books at their voting precinct. On behalf of these people, I argued that the law favored that election laws must be liberally construed to favor the policy of not denying one's right to vote.[29] This is especially true when administrative error by the state in failing to follow the law creates a barrier to voting.

Foregoing the legalese, if the Board of Elections or other administrative governmental agency may have been at fault for your name not being in a polling book (you signed a registration form and a voter registration group advised you it was being delivered to the Board of Elections), the right to vote is so sacred that you should be allowed to vote if you can present credible evidence that you followed proper registration procedures and the government messed up. Hello, same day registration laws anyone? Yes, for more than a third of our evolved states and D.C., all of whom understood that barriers to voters are anti-democratic, immoral and against a fundamental value of American citizenship – the right to vote in free and fair elections.[30] Maybe one day the rest of the country will move into the age of enlightenment and make voting easy, quick and fair. We need not discuss the idiotic, unsubstantiated and dishonest arguments about potential voter fraud which have been debunked, discredited and factually disproven beyond argument despite some politicians who peddle in lies to stop full voter participation.[31] Yes, you Donald and your sycophant elected enablers in the Republican Party (Not all. Just the many spineless and shameless flunkeys we all know.). That feels good to say. The truth sets us free.

As the morning wore on, I kept thinking about a fascinating legal argument that was contained in my preparation material distributed to me by the voter protection organization. It cited the federal National Voter Registration Act of 1993 and a similar New Jersey statute that, in essence, required motor vehicle offices as well as social service agencies (such as health service programs and public assistance benefit programs) to mandate that their clerks ask persons who visited such offices in person whether they wanted to register to vote while conducting business at the agencies. If the answer was yes, the agent was required to offer the member of the public a voter registration form to fill out, give back to the agent and the agent would be required to forward it to the appropriate Board of Elections.

I thought back to my own experiences at the motor vehicle department when renewing a license or registration in person. I never remember an agent asking me that question even though I now learned that it was a legal requirement. Since the intent of the law was to provide an easy opportunity for citizens to register to vote, I (and those who wrote the materials from which I learned) thought that was a potential gold mine as a legal argument for voters who were not in polling books as registered voters but who did visit such agencies. Once a potential voter credibly (meaning the judge believed she was telling the truth) established that she was not offered to register to vote at the agency, the burden should shift to the state as to why that wasn't done. If the voter credibly testified that if they were given such an opportunity to register that they would have, then they shouldn't be denied their right to vote due to an agency's failure to follow the law and register them.

I thought it was a very sound and fair argument so when the day began I asked all voters showing up for the hearings to show me their licenses and tell me when they last went to the DMV or a social services agency and whether they were offered a voter registration form and if not, would they have filled it out and given it back to the agent if so offered.

42

I felt the law was very clear that a voter should not be denied her right to vote because of a government employee's error in not following the law that was intended to make voter registration simple, quick and completed on the spot. Those brilliant prep materials were really onto something.

I represented dozens of voters during the course of my 14-hour day before two different judges. While each judge started out skeptical about my argument, I cited the applicable federal and state statutes as well as applicable New Jersey law. I prepared a very cogent and crisp direct examination the night before (the hearing rarely lasted more than 10 minutes) and my re-cross (after the Republican Party attorney and the Assistant Attorney General did their questioning in favor of denying the voter's right to vote) followed the facts that came out on the voter's cross-examination.

While the judges at first found the argument novel (It was creative and legally sound thanks to some superb attorneys who fashioned the argument in the voter protection notebook.) they respected that it had a solid legal and factual foundation grounded in federal and state law.

I was thrilled, proud and so excited that the judges found almost all of "my" voters (when I represent you I am 100% all in as a protector of your legal rights so I use the term "my" with great affection) credible in their testimony about their experiences at the motor vehicle offices and social services agencies. They had clearly been denied their right to register due to governmental error in failing to ask them if they wanted to register as required by law. Therefore, they were denied their right to vote through the fault of governmental failure, not through any fault of their own. The judges ruled in favor of my voters in almost every case and the previously disenfranchised voters took their court orders back to the polling places and cast their votes.

What a great day for democracy. What a great day for voting rights. What a great day for a few dozen citizens who were so offended and appalled by being told by a poll worker they were not registered to vote and not be allowed to vote, that they made a monumental effort to drive to the county seat, present their written denial to the Board of Elections, get ushered across the street into a courtroom, have a volunteer attorney like me represent them after some private questioning and testify at a hearing before a trial judge to get their right to vote restored.

Every one of those citizens was a hero to me. They felt targeted. They felt wronged. They knew their basic American right to vote was under attack. I am sure there were many others that day in polling places nationwide who accepted the on the spot decision of the poll worker denying them their right to cast their ballot and went home or back to work without voting. These people of great conviction that I represented were having none of that.

A poll worker was going to stop them from voting? The precious right to vote was not going to be taken away from them in an instant. People died fighting for the right to vote. No one should ever forget that fact. Slavery. Jim Crow laws. The Woman's Suffrage Movement. The new wave of voter "challengers" disproportionately involving people of color. It is a sordid, ugly and vile history and it still exists in different forms throughout the country. But on Election Day in 2005 in a courthouse in New Jersey I participated in the resistance along with my voters. Resistance to making a mockery of the right to vote. Resistance to erecting barriers to the right to vote. Resistance to disproportionate challenges to African-Americans whose right to vote has been at the core of their struggle for equality for 400 years. Hell yes. Resistance is a great thing. Those voters in Bergen County stood up and were counted. They resisted. I and other pro bono lawyers stood tall with them, represented them and resisted an attack, whether intentional, unintentional or systemic, on voting rights in America. Resistance feels really good by the way.

I felt so triumphant and energized despite the 13-hour shift. I felt like in my small corner of the voting universe I made a real difference. Most importantly, those voters walked away with the knowledge that equal justice can be done, there are lawyers and judges who care deeply about justice for all and these voters' courageous perseverance paid off with a vote cast on a day when they were told by a poll worker they were being denied the right to vote. What a fantastic day unfolded during my first round of voter protection hearings as the hours passed. Yes, to vote is the ultimate act of resistance. Never forget that all policies and laws flow from those whom you vote for or against.

Alas, that day in 2005 was just another beginning in this journey. You didn't think the Republican lawyers who opposed every voter I represented (they had the absolute right to take that legal position) were just going to accept this rash of voters actually being allowed to vote in the off-year election of 2005 that they believed were not properly registed? Especially since off-year elections in New Jersey still mean gubernatorial elections every 4 years. In 2005, it meant a victory for Democrat Jon Corzine for governor. Yay! 2006 would be another story with congressional seats, a senate seat and local/state elections in full bloom. Read on.

CHAPTER FOUR

2006:

THE REPUBLICANS ARE ONTO ME AND THE GREAT LEGAL ARGUMENT FASHIONED BY THE DEMOCRATIC ELECTION PROTECTION TEAM

My committee heads at the Democratic Voter Protection Team in Bergen County were extremely pleased at my results and the use of that motor vehicle agency/social services agency argument that the judges most often ruled in favor of because it was, I believe, right under the law. The Republican lawyers were not so happy with it. Just basing that on them arguing virtually every time against my voter being allowed to vote. This next comment is not directed to my Republican adversaries who ethically took a different legal position than me. I'll never understand how denying people the right to vote is a goal by anyone in a democracy, but then again I never understood how anyone could oppose the legality and morality of civil rights, voting rights and human rights; even more so when those rights are denied disproportionately to African-Americans throughout history and into the present.

So now Election Day 2006 is approaching and I am really gung-ho on a repeat performance in court in New Jersey. The law hasn't changed in New Jersey. The judges will be different, but hopefully open. The numbers of aggrieved voters will probably increase since there are Senate and House seats at stake in addition to local and state elections. I've waited a whole year for this and I am more prepared than ever.

I have signed up for the same 13-hour shift and can barely sleep with anticipation of another banner day restoring people's faith in voting, democracy and the court system. I come in like I'm shot out of a cannon. Most courtrooms have multiple attorneys on the Democratic side arguing cases alternatively. Most of the volunteer lawyers are not trial attorneys so they are not particularly comfortable in a hearing setting which is really a mini-trial with short openings, direct-examination, cross-examination, re-cross examination, closing arguments and case law/statutory arguments to the judge (no jury). Due to my love of trials, I ask the other lawyers in the 2 courtrooms that I was in that day to let me argue the hearings and have them do the initial interviews of the voters as they are brought into the courtroom so I can know the basic facts to prepare my questions before I have a quick Q&A with the voter. All of the lawyers oblige since they have excellent client interviewing skills and I come off like a guy who lives and eats the trial work. Everyone is happy. Everyone wins.

The day starts off fine. I have refined my motor vehicle department/social services department arguments from last year. Once again these become the vast majority of my voters' fact patterns and legal arguments. There is a sprinkling of other registration issues but they require less nuance and are less subject to interpretation by the judge. The same arguments from 2005 dominate the fact patterns testified to by the voters and the judge is very receptive to the argument.

Just indulge me in a little legalese for a moment. We live in a country which was built on striving to uphold the principles of fairness, justice and participatory democracy. All of those require the free and fair exercise of the right to vote so the will of the people will prevail through duly elected representatives from the local school board official to the President of the United States. A famous New Jersey case capsuled the reason why reasonable legal arguments favoring voters became so well received by the Bergen County judges in 2006 and 2007:

"We premise our holding upon the fundamental precept that 'the exercise of the basic right of suffrage, a civil and political franchise ... [is] of the very essence of our democratic *232 process.' Gangemi v. Berry, 25 N.J. 1, 12, 134 A.2d 1 (1957). As Justice Francis noted in Asbury

Park Press, Inc. v. Woolley, 33 N.J. 1, 11, 161 A.2d 705 (1960), 'No man can boast of a higher privilege than the right granted to the citizens of our State and Nation of equal suffrage and thereby to equal representation in the making of the laws of the land.' Because the right to vote is the bedrock upon which the entire structure of our system of government rests, our jurisprudence is steadfastly committed to the principle that election laws must be liberally construed to effectuate the overriding public policy in favor of the enfranchisement of voters."[32]

The courts, at least in New Jersey (I can't speak for the U.S. Supreme Court after Bush v. Gore), understood the rarefied space that voting rights occupy in this country. Contorted rules of voter registration and other artificial barriers (I'll get to those later) that deny voting rights are at best arcane and are at worst intentional means of obstruction by insidious political forces targeting specific groups (sadly, it is consistently African-Americans and other people of color) whose general voting patterns do not favor their politics. This is why courts are the last bastion to protect the right to vote when state legislatures and Congress fail. I am very proud to be a member of a profession from which the ranks come judges who understand their solemn duty to uphold the right to vote and interpret election law with a view toward favoring the right to vote over the denial of the right to vote as long as someone is at least 18 years of age and a U.S. Citizen. Any other view of voting rights law misconstrues what it means to be a fair, just and democratic country.

All right, back to the action in 2006. The crowds were forming. The voters turned away from the polls for alleged failed registration were coming to court and the battle was on. As usual, the Republican lawyers were on the side of denying voters the right to vote (I impute no particular motive to them other than my observation was that their legal argument was always to deny the particular voter the right to vote). Also as usual, the vast majority of the voters coming to court to restore their right to vote in Bergen County were African-American voters. There was the potential disparate impact on African-American voters.[33]

The morning court session was humming along. I was piling up victories with the Motor Vehicle Commission "administrative failure to offer voter registration as mandated by law" argument that I used the year before. I was beaming with pride for all of the voters who marched in the courtroom as disenfranchised voters and marched out with court orders restoring their right to vote that day. Votes would be cast. Votes would be counted. It doesn't get better than that on Election Day. Or so I thought.

The Republican lawyers were huddling in the hallway as their losses mounted (Their losses were voters wins. Go figure.). I noticed the head honcho Republican lawyer who never showed up at hearings all of a sudden was sitting in on some of my hearings in the late morning and early afternoon. Something was up and it wasn't going to be pretty.

A little after 1:00 PM the judge signed another order in its usual form that the court "being satisfied that the applicant is a qualified voter and entitled under applicable law to vote . . . that the voter is permitted . . .to cast his/her vote on the voting machine designated for that district." The Republican lawyers had now had enough of me and the winning Democratic lawyers' legal arguments. They applied for and received a stay of that order (meaning a particular voter was not allowed to vote) until the appeals court heard oral argument of the trial judge's order allowing the woman to vote.

Wow. I really ticked them off. Now I was a victim of my own success. They wanted to use this particular hearing and order as a test case to get an appeals court to rule that the whole administrative agency argument was a sham, an unlawful way around voter registration laws. Do you believe that? They got upset that too many Americans were being allowed to vote. In a country that reaches only about 60% turnout in presidential election years and 40% in midterm elections, the Republican lawyers were challenging what I and multiple trial judges believed to be a reasonable legal argument that resulted in an increase in votes cast by people who were eligible voters.[34] **Voting must be the ultimate act of resistance, otherwise why would one party (Hi Republicans) be so intent on limiting it?** And why would limiting it most often disproportionately affect African-Americans who historically vote in large numbers for Democrats? I leave those obvious answers to you. I specifically am not imputing any bad motive to the particular lawyers I faced in court that day (they had a right to argue a different interpretation of the law).

When I told my headquarters that oral argument before the appeals court was scheduled via telephone for early afternoon, they immediately understood the importance of the appellate argument and subsequent ruling. It would either put an end to our very successful legal argument or it would allow it to continue without further obstruction. Either way it would be precedent-setting for this county and the other counties throughout New Jersey where it was also being used in voting rights hearings throughout the state.

You need to understand that the powers that be in the Democratic voter protection group I worked for were a tightly-knit group of local lawyers who practiced in that county and before the appellate division all the time. While I have always been licensed in New Jersey and maintain a satellite office there, I have been based in Manhattan and practicing before the courts in New York City since 1982. None of these lawyers knew me before 2005 and even then, they only saw my results, but barely had contact with me. It was the same in 2006.

When I told them the news of the appeal, they told me they would be handling the oral argument before the appellate judge. I not only try my own cases involving personal injury/medical malpractice/civil rights in New York City, as well as trying cases for other firms that retain me as trial counsel, I also do my own appeals as well as appeals for other law firms. There was no way I was letting some other lawyer argue an appeal on an issue near and dear to my heart. No one knew how that hearing went except me. It was my baby and I was not going to let it out of my arms. The Democratic Party honchos were not happy with my stance, but they did understand no one else knew the case and legal arguments like me since I was the one doing battle on this case and similar cases for 2 Election Days in a row. Dozens of hearings. Dozens of wins. Now it was showtime in the appellate division and I would have grabbed the phone away from another Democratic lawyer during oral argument if I had to (Just joking. Maybe not.).

They felt my fervor and passion and knew up until then I had never failed them. They recognized my seriousness of purpose. They knew I would be totally prepared. They also were very concerned that the biggest appeal of our most successful legal argument was being handed over to a guy they really didn't know and wasn't part of their club. To their great credit, they trusted me, held their breath and handed over the reins of the appeal to me.

I recall that the oral argument by teleconference was made by a lawyer from the State Republican organization (I guess they understood the statewide precedent at stake and took it away from the county lawyers), a lawyer from the State Attorney General's office and me. As in all appellate arguments, we all got peppered with questions and the judge's reaction gave no indication as to which way she was going to rule. I really cannot recall who, but I believe one of the higher ups in the county Democratic organization was sitting nearby anxiously listening to the oral arguments. It was tense. It was fast. It was the real deal.

So? You think I wrote this book to tell you how I blew it for the Democratic Party statewide in New Jersey? We won. Of course. The order of the trial judge was affirmed and the voter was given her order to vote. The argument about administrative failure was now tested on appeal and the right to vote was favored over the denial of the right to vote based on the law and facts of our case. Don't forget, the judge in each individual case has to find that my voter is credible, telling the truth and the events happened as she said in order to succeed on our legal argument. That's why we don't win every time because not every witness is believed by the particular judge (That's what they get paid for – to judge.).

I truly was on cloud 9. What started as a few court hearings on election morning 2005, now blossomed into dozens of voters having their rights restored and an appellate court telling me and the Republican lawyers that the legal arguments of the Democrats are reasonable, valid and in conformance with the law.

The supervising attorneys back at headquarters were beyond ecstatic. They were generous with their praise and

I was very grateful for the opportunity that they gave me to argue the appeal. I am positive that they were very anxious leaving the fate of their well-crafted legal argument in my hands before the appellate division. They were rewarded for their confidence and trust. This was my form of resistance to letting anyone else argue "my" voter's case.

There was no time to celebrate. I immediately went back into a different courtroom and argued (mostly successfully) another dozen or so cases until the polls closed at 8:00 PM. When the new judge (different than my morning assignment) initially questioned my agency argument, I waved my appellate order in the air and advised him that this argument is settled law today. He got to make the factual findings and credibility findings, but the law was now set in the voter's favor.

I have fortunately had many highs in my legal career as a trial attorney in New York City. It is always an honor to represent my clients whether the case is a construction accident, a police brutality/civil rights case or a medical malpractice lawsuit. Added to those moments was Election Day 2006. I saw so many of my voters persist and win back their right to vote during the hearings. The special bonus was that the appellate court said that our legal argument is right. The winner that day was the sacred right to vote. The winners were those citizens who wouldn't accept a poll worker's words, "you cannot vote today". They found their way to court and they found their right to vote was just a court order away. That's what really makes America great.

CHAPTER FIVE

2008:

A Brave Woman Teaches a Judge
a Lesson in the Law

———————

I remember canvassing door to door with my wife and brother in Allentown, Pennsylvania in the fall of 2008. We were so excited about the candidacy of Barack Obama. So smart. So inspirational. So right on the issues. Our first African-American Presidential nominee. So right for the times.

The country was entering a deep financial crisis. We had been in two wars for years. Dick Cheney was still running the country into the ground as Bush looked as bewildered as ever. It was a particularly critical election about the future and John McCain looked so yesterday. He had the audacity to pick Sarah Palin for vice president, a candidate who didn't know much about anything. It was a nightmare scenario if Obama was not elected.

But was a country steeped in centuries of troubled racial history ready to elect its first African-American president? I believed America was ready, but it wouldn't be easy. The roar of the conservatives was loud. The never-ending voices of racism were loud. The polls seemed fairly good but who really knew?

My biggest concern was voter suppression. If the 2000 and 2004 elections were filled with incidents of voting irregularities, intimidation and systemic problems disproportionately affecting African-American voters, what would be in store for the potential election of our first African-American president? Unimaginable on one level, but totally predictable given recent history.

I would not be able to travel on Election Day out-of-state due to obligations of my law practice, but I was pleased to go back to court hearings in Bergen County. I imagined that the Republicans who took their lumps in the 2006 hearings and appeal would be particularly fired up for this election. Obama was portrayed as too liberal, too inexperienced and too. . . I'm too polite to say it, but you know what some conservatives were thinking. They questioned his birthplace, his religion and his allegiance to his country. I knew this Election Day was going to be on another level. Not a good level.

To deny the conspiracy theories were race-based is to deny the reality of hundreds of years of racism in America. Obviously, one could have a reasonable political difference with Obama's proposed policies. That was totally legitimate.

That was not the basis for the vile conspiracy theories surrounding his candidacy. We know how they derived, we know why they derived and we know the kinds of people who trafficked in that cesspool of character assassination. I was as disgusted by it as were most reasonable Americans in 2008, but I looked at it from another perspective as well. What lengths would the haters go to in suppressing the vote, especially the African-American vote? I went into the 2008 voter protection hearings in court with a laser focus on the historic nature of the election and the unprecedented obstruction that voters might face at the polls. As ready as I always was for my court hearings, I was particularly wound up in 2008. Election Day could not come fast enough for me. I knew the Republican lawyers would be at the top of their game. They had suffered some big court losses and election losses in the past, but this was different. After 8 years of Republican rule, Republican Supreme Court appointments and Republican conservatives in charge, the Democrats had a real chance to take the Presidency along with the House and Senate. The stakes were high, they knew it and we knew it. It felt like a lead up to a heavyweight championship fight in October. It was November so I heard the proverbial "let's get ready to rumble" in my head on Election Day morning.

In the preparation meeting, I received some excellent news about that motor vehicle argument that I had used so many times which was upheld on appeal in 2006. I always understood through my own experiences and the testimony of voters that the Motor Vehicle Commission was not complying with the mandate for agents to offer all customers voter registration applications. Everything that the voters said and the judges accepted as credible was confirmed by the Department of the Public Advocate of New Jersey in 2007 in real time:

> "In February 2007, the Public Advocate sent personnel to 11 MVC agencies throughout New Jersey to survey customers whose just-completed transactions at MVC should have triggered motor vehicle activities. However, out of 494 individuals surveyed, only eight percent said they were offered the opportunity to register to vote. . . These findings mirror those of the U.S. Election Assistance Commission (EAC), which has consistently ranked New Jersey close to last compared to other states in the percentage of registrations conducted at motor vehicle agencies. On average, motor vehicle offices accounted for half of all new voter registrations nationwide in 2005 and 2006. However, in New Jersey, the MVC accounted for only 92,890 of the 808,794 total new voter registration applications submitted in the State, or about 11 percent."[35]

Every bit of testimony from those voters I represented in 2005-2007 was now verified by this study. 8% compliance? That is such a poor performance especially when it affected so many citizens' right to vote. Those legal arguments made by me and many other Democratic lawyers now seemed stronger than ever. The whole point of the 1993 "Motor Voter Act" was to require "motor vehicle agencies to offer citizens an expedited and easy opportunity to register to vote when they obtain or renew a driver's license or non-driver's identification card."[36]

Real change came as a result of those court hearings and the efforts of the Public Advocate (Many times attorneys for that office were present in court arguing the same position as the Democratic voter protection attorneys. They were very well informed and cooperative at all times.). The Public Advocate, the New Jersey Motor Vehicle Commission and the Attorney General's office in 2008 (prior to Election Day) had reached a "Memorandum of Understanding" (legalese for an agreement) wherein:

"MVC agents – will hand "short form" voter registration applications to all customers; collect and forward completed forms from those who choose to register; post signs informing the public about their right to register at MVC agencies; and train MVC employees about these obligations.

In addition, the MVC and the Division of Elections will make sure that address changes made at the MVC are transferred to the appropriate election databases and will reach out to former MVC customers who are not registered to vote to offer them a chance to register. To ensure compliance with the commitment, the MVC will conduct random compliance inspections at MVC offices and will post compliance rates on its website."[37]

This was an incredibly important and major step to avoid voters being turned away from the polls who were told they were not registered but were really not registered solely because of MVC agents' failure to offer them registration. No citizen should be denied the right to vote because a state agency failed in its duty to offer, assist and register the voter as required by law.

While the changes would not happen for large numbers of voters for some time, they should eventually dramatically increase voter registration at the Motor Vehicle Commission offices, an agency where a very large number of potential voters appear in person at regular intervals. It would take years to make a big difference since citizens only go for renewals a number of years apart, but eventually the problem would be mostly eliminated.

That's the good news. The bad news is that it wouldn't have an immediate effect on the 2008 election where turnout was expected to be very high.

On Election Day 2008 from the beginning of the morning until after the polls closed (as long as you are in line when the polls close you have the right to cast your ballot), it felt like non-stop hearings in all of the open courtrooms. Once again it was a high concentration of African-American and some Latino (a very small percentage of white people as usual) voters who had been denied their right to vote and showed up in court to argue for restoration of their right to vote before a judge.

This day felt different early on. The voters were very intense and almost all of them mentioned how important it was for them to cast their vote in this particular election. As usual, I never inquired about who they supported, but almost every voter said today could be history and they must be a part of it (obviously referring to the potential election of our first African-American President, not a potential Alaskan vice-president who was not too good with geography or identifying her favorite reading materials). There was a palpable voter passion that made this an exciting and unique day in court. Hold on for the best story of the day.

Dozens and dozens of voters came through the two courtrooms in which I was arguing cases. The cases were coming fast and furious all day. The usual issues were arising and the usual legal arguments were being made. There were a number the voters who moved within the county to a new address within the county and were wrongly denied their right to vote requiring a court order after a hearing.

There were also many hearings on the issue of "good faith efforts" to register. These are cases wherein voters under penalty of perjury gave sworn testimony that they made a good faith effort to register to vote and believed that they were in fact registered. Especially in years like 2008 when many volunteer groups held voter registration drives, loads of previous unregistered voters signed voter registration applications at rallies, shopping malls and at sidewalk tables. These efforts are admirable and also valuable in increasing voter turnout. The new registrant relies on the volunteer organization to deliver the signed application to the proper Board of Elections office. Since the law favors enfranchisement (being able to vote) over disenfranchisement (taking away one's right to vote), if a voter testifies under oath in New Jersey that she signed a registration application and either mailed it or was advised a registration group would deliver it for her, the judge is left with making a decision as to the credibility (truthfulness) of the voter's intent to register. If she is believed but the election officials have no record of the registration, then the voter should be allowed to vote since she obviously made a "good faith effort" to register and through some administrative/postal/delivery error not of her own making the registration wasn't received and/or recorded in the Board of Elections' records. That is a very reasonable legal analysis since we should always favor voting over the denial of voting. Most judges recognize that basic principle and rule in favor of credible voters who made such efforts to register.

Then, of course, the motor vehicle registration cases consumed much of the hearing day for all of the lawyers working the hearings on Election Day 2008. Once someone produces a driver's license or non-driver's license MVC ID, it is clear when an in-person visit was made to a motor vehicle office. If the voter swears they were not offered the right to register to vote at that time, it was an agent of the state of New Jersey who failed to follow the "Motor Voter Act". We know from those studies cited before that the agents failed 92% of the time to follow the law in New Jersey in the 2007 sampling.[38] Those cases were again well received by most of the judges in 2008 especially with the citation to the above Public Advocate's study and the further data that New Jersey ranked "close to last compared to other states in the percentage of registrations conducted at motor vehicle agencies".[39]

Based on courthouse chatter and an appellate decision order that I received later in the day, there was a judge in the building hearing cases who was either not familiar with the "Motor Voter Act" legal argument or chose to ignore it. Her failure to adhere to the law led to an appeal by a voter on Election Day who was apparently not allowed to be questioned about his appearance at the motor vehicle office, whether he was offered a voter registration and whether he would have registered had he been so offered the opportunity. The appellate judge spelled it out for the Superior Court in her order. The appellate court ordered the Superior Court judge to question the voter as above and if the trial court judge determines that the answers are credible, then it must order the voter be allowed to vote if the credible answers were in the affirmative or deny the right to vote if the credible answers were in the negative. It was a travesty that two years after my similar case went to the Appellate Division, again a voter was improperly denied the right to vote without a full and fair opportunity at a proper hearing. This is why we have appellate courts. Lower court judges don't always do the right thing under the law for a variety of reasons. Justice triumphed once again.

As the afternoon turned into evening the post-work rush began. The courthouse was literally overflowing with voters who had been denied their right to vote in an election for the ages. The hearings were voluminous and contentious in the afternoon as I was appearing before a judge highly skeptical of voter testimony and apparently (my inference only) not especially in favor of the public policy favoring enfranchisement over disenfranchisement.

This particular judge was stern, curt and not particularly open to the legal arguments that had been accepted as persuasive and fair by most other judges on Election Day 2005, 2006 and 2008. To be clear, she has an absolute right to call them as she sees them whether I agree or disagree. (I am certainly not making any accusations that she did anything beyond the scope of her rightful discretion.). She was also not overly pleased with the crowd forming which meant that we would be working well past the poll closing hour of 8:00 PM. While the judge was presented with many "Motor Voter Act" arguments by me on behalf of voters, she was very skeptical about the testimony. She was very quick to not believe the testimony. It took herculean efforts to get her to conceive that the testimony was credible. She obviously did not like the basis of the "Motor Voter Act" arguments, but knew she was duty bound to follow the law. However, she was the fact-finder so if she did not believe the voter's story about not being offered a registration application at the MVC, she had a right to reject the testimony and deny the person the right to vote. She did it on a number of occasions and other times she was left no choice since the facts, the license information and the demeanor of the witness made the decision to favor the voter inescapable. She really seemed distrustful of most voters' sworn testimony. Not a good way for me to start each argument.

As I was making argument after argument for hours before her, the judge was very rigid. I won most hearings, but I lost some that I believe should have ended the other way. That is the life of a trial lawyer; no one wins them all and a judge is still a human in robes so things aren't always the way we like. I, of course, accept her authority even when I vehemently disagree with her ruling.

It was probably close to 7:00 PM and the courtroom was completely filled with lawyers, voters and court personnel. There was a feverish pitch to the proceedings since the polls were soon closing and the crowds were not stopping. Tension was the prevailing mood. Everyone felt it.

I turned around in my 12th hour on my feet and caught the eye of the next voter. She was a 23-year-old African-American woman. She seemed shy. She was very soft spoken. She was very nervous. I had my usual quick look at the voter's story prepared by another lawyer colleague in the back who interviewed her. She presented with a common set of facts. She had moved from one county to another and was not aware of the re-registration requirement. On that basis the judge would surely ban her from voting as did the local poll worker an hour before she drove to court. I gathered information about her experiences at the MVC office regarding voter registration. I then also got a little background information from her as was my custom to begin the argument.

Before I turned around to go back to the counsel table with her to begin the hearing, I looked in her eyes and they were so sad. I said, within earshot of others, "You really want to vote today, don't you?" With a trembling voice, that others close by could hear, she said "I have to vote today. We can have the first African-American President ever and I have to cast my vote for him. He is a special man. He needs me today". (These were not confidential discussions. They were made in an open area since they did not relate to her testimony or any confidential information.) She spoke with such conviction, purpose and heart. I just couldn't lose this hearing. She was counting on me to get her right to vote back so she could cast a vote that she had obviously dreamt about with pride and passion. I couldn't let this judge break this young woman's heart and spirit on a day so important to her.

I went through my usual direct examination with this woman and she answered very credibly in her soft-spoken tone. It sounded like very honest testimony to me. The cross-examination by the Republican lawyer was the usual and nothing he asked revealed any contradictions in her testimony. I was now bracing for the judge to ask her own questions which she had done regularly during the afternoon when she was preparing to deny my application (My interpretation. I want to be clear I respect judges and that is her lawful province to ask questions.). What happened next was appalling then exhilarating, then, you'll read on for the ending.

The judge ripped into this pleasant woman in open court with great skepticism The judge said in a raised and accusatory voice, "What's wrong with you? Are you so unaware that you don't know the voter registration laws that require you to re-register when you move to another county?" The woman responded that she did not know the law. The young woman was visibly shaken and the courtroom volume turned to a hush as the judge's voice grew angrier. She said, "You don't know anything about voting. Weren't you taught about voting at home or in high school? How did you find out about registering the first time when you said you did it at 18?" The woman responded, "I was in my high school and I saw a group of people waiting in line in the gym and going into these booths set up with curtains. I didn't have any idea what they were doing. When one of them walked out of the gym I asked her what she was doing. She said she had just voted. I really didn't know exactly what she meant. It was never talked about in my home or among my friends and family. So I asked this nice woman a lot of questions and she told me all about voting. It sounded very important and something I needed to do when I turned 18. She explained to me it was my duty as a citizen and that things could only change when we vote for people who will change things. I then spoke to one of my teachers about it and soon after I was given a voter registration application by her since I had just turned 18 and I filled it out and mailed it in. Since that day I have voted in every election and understood how important it is."

Everyone in that courtroom could feel the sincerity and earnestness in her voice. Well, almost everyone. The judge was unimpressed and came back at her with a scowl and in a booming voice berated her again before a filled courtroom, "I don't' really care about your high school years. I care about the law. You violated the law. You shouldn't be allowed to vote because you are irresponsible and had no interest in learning about the law of re-registration. You don't deserve to vote and that story about the motor vehicle office, it sounds fishy to me." The woman's eyes filled with tears as her body trembled. She was not just feeling humiliated in open court for fighting to restore her right to vote, she was being denied her dream of casting a vote for our first African-American President. She looked at me with desperate eyes and a silent plea to turn this nightmare around. Everything I believed in about the sacredness of voting was on the line and was embodied in this woman's battle for her right to vote.

I told you it was appalling. It was uncalled for. It seemed mean-spirited. While the judge was within her rights to address a litigant in a manner she saw fit, I felt it was unnecessary and unbecoming of a judge who takes an oath to uphold the laws, not berate well-meaning citizens. At that moment, I thought back to that elderly African-American woman in Cleveland who experienced the blatant racism of the Jim Crow South in Mississippi and told me not to worry about her, no one was taking away her right to vote. "Just go out and help the others who haven't seen what I've seen." Now was the moment that wise woman was talking about.

The judge was ready to give her decision and I knew it was going to a bad place. In my extensive preparations for these hearings over the years, I had read and re-read the law and remembered a passage that I had never had the need to cite before this moment. This judge set the stage for a dramatic moment.

Just as the judge was about to render her order denying this woman the right to vote, I turned to the judge in a forceful but respectful voice that boomed for all to hear, "Judge, I respectfully request to be heard on one more issue before you render your decision." I pulled out a copy of the federal law known as the "National Voter Registration Act of 1993" (the "Motor Voter Act" that I used as a general basis for my many arguments in 2005-2008) and read the preamble out loud to the judge:

"The Congress finds that--

(1) the right of citizens of the United States to vote is a fundamental right;

(2) it is the duty of the Federal, State, and local governments to promote the exercise of that right; and

(3) discriminatory and unfair registration laws and procedures can have a direct and damaging effect on voter participation in elections for Federal office and disproportionately harm voter participation by various groups, including racial minorities.

(b) Purposes.--The purposes of this Act are—

(1) to establish procedures that will increase the number of eligible citizens who register to vote in elections for Federal office;

(2) to make it possible for Federal, State, and local governments to implement this Act in a manner that enhances the participation of eligible citizens as voters in elections for Federal office;

(3) to protect the integrity of the electoral process; and

(4) to ensure that accurate and current voter registration rolls are maintained."[40]

I said "Judge, this act was specifically written by Congress for this young woman. It specifically refers to racial minorities of which she is clearly a member. Actually, she is an African-American, a group whose entire voting rights history is filled with bloodshed, Jim Crow laws and other means of voter suppression. Congress found it important enough to specify whose rights this law was meant to protect – hers. It clearly states that this law was enacted to increase voter registration and enhance participation of eligible citizens in elections for federal office. When Congress is so clear about its motive I believe no state or federal court is empowered to override the intent of a duly enacted law – the intent to make sure a woman who is a member of a group whose right to vote has been denied and obstructed for centuries does not only have her rights protected but she is entitled to have her voting rights made easier by the procedures mandated in this 'Motor Voter Act'. If the authors of this bill were in this courtroom today, they would surely say, Judge we wrote this bill for this woman. She is our model of a citizen who took the initiative to register at age 18 once she learned about the value of voting from a fellow voter. She has voted in every election since then. She is working hard at a minimum wage job as she is moving

73

toward obtaining higher education. She is so passionate about voting that she went from her job to her polling place to this courthouse because the fundamental right to vote is so precious and sacred to her. She should be applauded and rewarded for her commitment to good citizenship and perseverance to come here tonight to restore her right to vote. She lost that right through no fault of her own. A clerk at the MVC didn't follow our enacted federal law that required him to give her the opportunity to re-register in her new county when she renewed her license recently. She did everything right and the agent of the state did everything wrong. She should not be denied a fundamental right of every American citizen because of some bureaucrat's mistake. She is credible. She is believable. She is honest. She is the very person for whom Congress passed this law in 1993. She was 8 years old then and we are so proud to have made a law that protected her right to vote 15 years later. All her determination today to come before you at this late hour tells us that Congress was right when it wrote 'discriminatory and unfair registration laws and procedures can have a direct and damaging effect on voter participation'. No more. That damage should not happen to this admirable woman tonight. We as a nation made sure of that in 1993. Now Judge, respectfully it is your honor's duty to execute on Congress' intent tonight and order that this woman be sent back to that polling place to cast her ballot as she wishes. This is America and her right to vote is fundamental, precious and must be honored."

I felt a bit like my boyhood hero, Atticus Finch (*To Kill a Mockingbird*) when I finished. The other lawyer was silent. The judge was actually silent. My voter looked over to me with tears streaming down her eyes. The judge finally broke her silence with an abrupt ruling. "Fine. The court finds in favor of the voter but you need to be more responsible about voting laws in the future. Take this order and go back to your polling place to cast your ballot. Next." The judge, despite her harsh manner, deserves a lot of credit for listening to the argument and making a ruling that I believe was absolutely right under the law.

The woman sobbed, I cried, we hugged. She tightly embraced me and thanked me over and over again. I told her that was my job to get her right to vote back and she was a hero to me. I told her to get going quickly back to the polls and do her duty. She had such a big grin on her face. I knew I did something very important. It was one voter, but it felt like one million voters. It was one of the finest moments of my career. I still see her face as I write this. First the tremble. Then the tears. Then the smile while still shaking. I am sure Barack Obama would be very proud to know her vote for him was cast and counted despite the barriers put up that day to deny her right to vote.

The judge was not enamored with me the rest of that busy night, but to her credit my voters started getting what I considered a fairer shake than what she had been doing earlier in the afternoon and evening. I will never know what the judge was really thinking during that remarkable testimony by that young woman, but I know that the final result affected not just one voter but others who were present at the hearing. I had two Republican lawyers come up to me at the end of the evening to congratulate me on my oral argument on behalf of that woman. They admitted right was right and the judge treated my voter with such skepticism and outright contempt before ruling in her favor. It was a gratifying moment and more importantly justice prevailed when moments before an ugly inequity looked like it was about to emerge for a passionate voter who deserved the right result.

The rest of the evening went well past the time the polls closed at 8:00 PM, but it was an honor to keep representing voters who made the extra effort to drive to the courthouse to restore their right to vote. It was obvious by the crowds that this special day reflected the passion of 575,145 new voters who had registered in New Jersey in 2008 before the October 14th deadline.[41]

I finally left the courtroom, thoroughly exhausted yet completely exhilarated. Everything I dreamt about in 2000 as to how to forge an important role in protecting voting rights played out during the course of a historic day in American political history. Everything I learned from the late Dr. Raymond Gavins in his African-American history course about the vile history of voting rights denials to African-Americans from slavery to Reconstruction to Jim Crow to systemic voter suppression poured through my head and heart all day. All that I had learned from that brave woman in Cleveland who grew up with the vicious, racist barriers placed before her in the segregated South replayed in my mind. All of the preparation I received from excellent Democratic Party voting rights attorneys who prepared superb materials in Bergen County, New Jersey were the tools I carried with me all day. My career as a trial lawyer prepared me for the kind of legal research, preparation and think-on-your-feet oratory necessary to be the very best advocate I could be for people who would not have been properly heard without a zealous advocate. I felt so good for all I helped, but also good for all of those who would tell others about how the justice system actually worked for them in a vital way on a very important day. As I always tell my clients in my practice I cannot guarantee you justice, but I can guarantee you the opportunity at justice. I cannot guarantee you will win, but I can guarantee you I will give you every ounce of sweat, blood and skill I have to represent you. That is a promise I can proudly say I always keep.

So after my traditional run on the way home for very unhealthy but delicious comfort food, I was excited to see that my wife Florence and our sweet dog Sadie were bracing for history before the television set. The results were going very well for Senator Obama and all indications were that America was about to do the right thing on so many levels.

After midnight, Barack Obama, the President-elect by all projections, electrified Grant Park in Chicago and the rest of the world as he came to a microphone and uttered these words:

> "If there is anyone out there who still doubts America is a place where all things are possible; who still wonders if the dreams of our founders are alive in our time; who still questions the power of our democracy, tonight is your answer.
>
> It's the answer told by lines that stretched around schools and churches in numbers this nation has never seen; by people who waited three hours and four hours, many for the very first time in their lives, because they believed that this time must be different; that their voices could be that difference. . .
>
> This election had many firsts and many stories that will be told for generations. But one that's on my mind tonight is about a woman who cast her ballot in Atlanta. She's a lot like millions of others who stood in line to make their voice heard in this election except for one thing – Ann Nixon Cooper is 106 years old.
>
> She was born just a generation past slavery; a time when there were no cars on the road or planes in the sky; when someone like her couldn't vote for two reasons – because she was a woman and because of the color of her skin . . .
>
> And this year, in this election, she touched her finger to a screen, cast her vote, because after 106 years in

America, through the best of times and the darkest of hours, she knows how America can change. Yes, we can . . . and those who tell us we can't, we will respond with the timeless creed that sums up the spirit of a people; Yes We Can . . ."[42]

It was beyond eloquent, inspiring and deeply emotional. It was the best of America. It channeled the America we want, but not always the America we get. When he spoke about 106-year-old Ann Nixon Cooper, I could not help but think back to the nexus with that 90 year old woman in Cleveland in 2004 and that 23 year old woman in Bergen County, New Jersey on Election Day 2008. They are why we must never surrender to the evil forces of voter suppression. They are why we must never stop fighting against factions that put barriers in front of eligible voters to keep the vote down in African-American and Democratic leaning communities. Voting rights should never be about stopping people from voting because of the color of their skin or the party they belong to. Voting rights are human rights. They represent the right of a free people to choose their leaders as representatives to achieve their dreams, hopes and goals of a better life, a fairer life and a more just and equal society.

For those that think that denial of the right to vote doesn't affect them because they are of a different race or different political party than those that are normally targeted, I point you to the brilliant civil rights and voting rights activist Fannie Lou Hamer – one of the most important figures of the 20th century (though not given the credit she deserves by historians) – who put that thinking to rest many decades ago when she said that **"Nobody's free until everybody's free."**[43] This legend for the ages also left us with the immortal words, **"I am sick and tired of being sick and tired"**.[44] Keep that one in mind when November 2020 rolls around (I know the former quote is in the acknowledgment, but it can never be repeated enough times.).

I encourage any reader who has not read much about Fannie Lou Hamer to do so immediately. She is an icon in the voting rights and civil rights movement of the 1960's and she has been rightfully referred to by many as the "spirit of the Civil Rights movement". Her life, her work and her undying spirit is guaranteed to inspire anyone who believes in freedom, equality and the sanctity of the right to vote.

As the night turned into morning, my wife and I decided that we must become a part of history so we made plans to stand on the grounds of the National Mall on the Inauguration Day of President Obama on January 20, 2009 (I refer to it as being uninvited guests to the inauguration since there are no tickets for the field we stood on.). It was one of the most moving moments of our lives.

I could not describe to you how I felt on that Inauguration Day any better than I did back on January 22, 2009 in an email to friends entitled "Rebirth of the UNITED States of America":

"My wife Florence and I had the honor of witnessing the rebirth of the **UNITED** States of America on the sacred ground of the National Mall in Washington D.C.

That ground was once a slave market leaving the tragic stain of the cruelest, most inhumane and fundamentally undemocratic institution that ever lived on our soil.

We watched the son of an African father and a Caucasian Kansas mother take the oath of office as our first African-American President at long last.

Americans never say it can't be done. We figure out how to do it. Barack Obama figured out a way to create a rebirth of the **UNITED** States of America at a time when freedom, democracy and equality had taken a bad beating for eight painful years.

I knew that Senator Obama would defeat the undemocratic forces at the moment Sarah Palin and Rudy Giuliani ridiculed Barack Obama for having been a community organizer. Mocking community organizers is like mocking abolitionists, mocking suffragettes, mocking human rights advocates, mocking our soldiers or mocking free and fair elections. This outrageous anti-democratic fervor of the Bush years needed to stop under the leadership of former community organizer Barack Obama.

The salaried worker, struggling single mom and small businessman would not favor a party that held community organizers in contempt. Community organizers are the citizens who feed the homeless, re-train the unemployed, acclimate immigrants, build a high school arts program and protect minority rights from the tyranny of the majority. We are a people founded by community organizers like those who led the American Revolution and the Selma to Montgomery March.

America's number one community organizer did quite a job organizing his fellow citizens to get 53% of the electorate to support him. His spirit of community organizing touched the hearts, souls and passions of two million ordinary people to inspire us to stand in the dark and freezing cold from 4:45 a.m. until that magic moment at 12:00 p.m. to witness the glorious sun break through the clouds and welcome our 44th President on January 20th.

Our two days in D.C. were filled with human warmth, a commonality of purpose and deep patriotism.

As the moment arrived and he officially became President Obama, the tears, hugs and smiles of relief overtook two million of us on the National Mall. As the oath ended, our new friend Michelle (we met her sister, mother and her on the metro at 4:00 a.m. and quickly became a family of five on a blanket on the Mall) turned around and hugged me with tears streaming down her cheeks; tears of pride, joy and dreams fulfilled. Her African-American heritage, Kansas roots and Brooklyn home all spoke in those tears. I knew the country I love was going to be fine again.

America is rededicating itself to our ideals of truth, justice, equality, freedom and compassion; living the dreams of Dr. King, President Lincoln and our founding fathers; reaching heights that dreamers could not imagine. Barack Obama has more than a dream. He has reality. He will make it happen because two million people on the Mall will walk with him, serve with him and join with 298 million other people to fulfill the reality of national ideals.

Unbridled success for America and the world is our only option because that is who we are. We are not torturers. We are not shadow governments. We are not bullies. We are all community organizers honor bound to preserve a more perfect union and fulfill the dreams of every freedom-loving person that came before us and will come after us. We are America. We are proud to lead the world into this era of rebirth. We welcome our friends in every corner of the world to join us in this march of community organizers. The national and international community now has a leader to organize us. President Obama is ready. America is ready. The world is ready."

CHAPTER SIX

2012 PHILADELPHIA:
"POLICE, POLICE, ARREST THAT MAN.
HE WANTS PEOPLE TO VOTE."

In 2009-2011, I continued my Election Day voter protection work in New Jersey with similar legal arguments and results akin to years past. It was always rewarding. It was always an honor to represent "my" voters. I need to add that in all my years of doing voter protection court hearings, I followed my principles in protecting everyone's right to vote. While I never asked people who they supported on the ballot, that didn't stop them from blurting it out anyway. A tiny (I mean especially tiny) number of the voters denied the right to vote at a polling place were self-identified Republican voters. I defended their right to vote with the same zeal and legal arguments I did for every other voter I represented. My Republican lawyer colleagues, not so much with self-identified Democratic voters. Actually, they never took the right to vote position for self-identified Democrats in my presence.

It did seem well beyond a coincidence that the only time the Republican lawyers in court defended the right to restore a voter's right to vote was when they either said aloud they were Republicans or they fit a demographic that the Republican lawyers may have assumed was not Democratic. I do not ascribe to them a bad motive, but I can state my observations were that in all of those years not one Republican adversary in court supported the position of restoring the voter's right to vote unless they were a self-identified Republican. I want to be very clear that I am in no way saying their motive was discriminatory or racist. Their position was what it was.

As 2012 rolled around I knew the re-election of President Obama was shaping up as a close contest. My trial schedule was more flexible in 2012 so I decided to pick a hot spot city where the Obama campaign needed me. It turned out to be a ride down the Jersey Turnpike to the historic and lovely city of Philadelphia (except for the Eagles since I am a diehard New York Giants fan). I was particularly interested in doing outside polling work in Philadelphia because of the potential for voter suppression arising from one of the most confusing court rulings in modern election law history.

It seemed to all lawyers and political junkies that paid attention that the Republicans realized by 2012 that voter ID laws (which often have a disparate impact on African-Americans, Latinos, lower income, disabled and student voters, i.e., predominantly Democratic voters) could help their transparent voter suppression efforts; they of course couched the ID laws as anti-voter fraud laws.[45] By 2012 only four states required photo ID for voters but the court challenges were getting mixed results.[46] A U.S. Supreme Court ruling in 2008 upholding Indiana's voter ID requirement was, in retrospect, an indicator of where the future of voting rights was heading.[47]

Pennsylvania in 2012 joined the voter disenfranchisement movement as some commentators have characterized it.[48] The State of Pennsylvania in March 2012 passed a law that required voters to show photo ID on Election Day 2012.[49] A lawsuit was brought by voting rights advocates on behalf of voters who would be disparately impacted and disenfranchised by the law.[50]

In a partial victory in September 2012, a judge ordered that with respect to the November 6th election, due to implementation issues arising in a short time before Election Day, the voter ID law was delayed until *after* the November 6, 2012 election. Voters will not be required to have ID at polling places, but poll workers can ask for ID nonetheless.[51] What? Are you kidding me? That just creates a climate for mayhem by poll workers who may intentionally or unintentionally ask for ID and tell voters it is required despite the opposite position of the court ruling. It sounded insane only because it was insane. Common sense informs us if the judge found the voter ID requirement should not be in effect on this particular Election Day, why allow poll workers to ask for it?

The attorneys in favor of the voting rights position immediately recognized the potential for a voter suppression bonanza on Election Day since the Commonwealth of Pennsylvania had already started an "education campaign" about bringing voter ID to the polls even though it was not required by the judge's decision.[52] The lawyers cited TV and radio ads, mailings and billboards that gave the public dangerous misinformation that voters were required to show photo ID at the polls on Election Day despite the court order to the contrary.[53] After the court order, there were literally billboards and bus ads that told voters they must show ID and then in much smaller font it stated "if you have it".[54] This was a textbook formula for voter confusion, voter suppression and an Election Day disaster at the polls. The court declined to issue a further order enjoining the disinformation campaign before Election Day.[55]

When I read about these reprehensible decisions in Pennsylvania, I knew I needed to be in Philadelphia to ensure a free and fair election was going to be held. I represented the Obama campaign in the voter rich, populous city of Philadelphia which needed a high turnout of the Obama base of African-Americans, Latinos and young voters. I got so much more than I bargained for as you can tell by the heading of this chapter.

2012 was a strange year. In late October, Hurricane Sandy had slammed the northeast, especially New York City and New Jersey. The damage was devastating. My apartment lost electricity from the storm as did my elderly parents' house nearby. As a result, we scrambled for a hotel as the mild fall weather turned wintry. It was a struggle convincing them to leave their beloved house (I literally said to them as my final argument, "I refuse to end up on the front page of the *New York Post* with a headline 'Son Allows Parents to Freeze to Death in Home without Heat'"). It was quite a struggle finding a vacant hotel with electricity. On the Saturday before Election Day I finally found one and made a reservation by phone at a motel nearby, packed everyone up and headed to our new temporary home until electricity was restored.

Of course, the best laid plans do not always pan out. When we arrived at the motel the parking lot seemed oddly empty for a refuge from the blackout ongoing in much of our area. When I walked in alone to check-in, I noticed no lights on in the lobby which was the telltale sign of a gigantic blunder. The desk clerk explained to me that they too had no electricity and the national reservation phone center I spoke with should have so advised me. That was all well and good but my elderly parents and wife were sitting in the car and we had no place to go. I really had to scramble to make things happen.

Fortunately, after many calls I hit on a nice hotel (I used the local phone number this time) that had two available rooms in Jersey City. I snatched them before the clerk finished his sentence. We drove directly to this lovely hotel steps from the Hudson River. It was such a stroke of good luck since they had a dining room so we didn't even have to figure out meals. It was 72-hours before Election Day so I was still on schedule to be in Philadelphia on Monday.

I had finished my online Pennsylvania voter protection training which, of course, emphasized the recent court rulings that were expected to confuse voters and poll workers alike. Fortunately, the electricity came back on in our homes on Monday morning and I drove everyone back to their abodes then I headed straight for my hotel in Philadelphia.

I didn't have any time to do canvassing in Philadelphia but did have an Obama Campaign invite later in the day to see Bill Clinton speak in person at the University of Pennsylvania. I was going to reward myself for a rough week by attending the indoor campaign rally.

The wait on campus turned out to be hours, but I had plenty of voter protection preparation materials on me to read during the wait. As the line proceeded into the arena, you had to decide to break left or right to the seats. I broke to the less crowded side of the line by instinct and that was the move of the day. I found myself standing on the gym floor about 10 feet from the podium. As the preliminary speakers gave their campaign pep talks, I realized how close I would be to President Clinton's speech. I had seen him speak one time before in 1992 at a New Jersey campaign rally but my brother and I were basically in the cheap seats very distant from then candidate Clinton. Not this time.

I knew President Clinton had a reputation for making everyone in the room feel like he was speaking to them. I can assure you that is not hyperbole. It is reality. When he spoke, I really felt like he was speaking to an audience of one. Maybe I imagined the eye contact with him, but it sure seemed real. He was magical. He was inspiring. He was as charismatic a person as I had ever seen or heard in person. The speech to a mostly college age crowd was a rousing endorsement not just of President Obama, but it spoke directly to the role of young people in the electoral process. He surely reached them as each word was mesmerizing to the young crowd. Most of the students were either not born or toddlers when he was first elected President but they hung on his every utterance. His charm, intelligence and connection with the audience were awe-inspiring. It was the perfect way to put a difficult week behind me and gear up for an expectedly tough day of election protection.

I was assigned to a polling place at a church in South Philadelphia. As you may recall, I went to the polling place at the housing project in Cleveland to introduce myself the day before to the project manager and some residents. They were welcoming and delightful. When I drove by the church on Monday evening, I didn't see anyone to speak with so I just figured it was best to come back early the next morning for an introduction since I would be outside the polls 7:00 AM to 8:00 PM. At least in my head that sounded reasonable.

My observation of the neighborhood on Monday evening was that it was quite diverse. I was hoping the polling personnel would be as friendly as the property manager and housing project residents in Cleveland. I would soon find out that was not happening.

I arrived extremely early on Election Day morning and waited in my car until I saw poll workers begin to arrive to open the polling station. After they went inside and long before the 7:00 AM opening time, I went inside to introduce myself as someone who would be working as a poll observer outside the polls and I made it very clear to them I understood the 100-foot rule (no electioneering or campaigning within 100 feet of the polling place entrance) and I would always stay 100 feet away from the poll entrance. The reception I got was a precursor to how the day was going to unfold.

My first reaction came from a poll worker who literally screamed at me to get out of the church. I calmly explained to her who I was and she continued to scream. In an attempt to keep things civil, I politely asked her if I could use the restroom in the church to which she replied, "No". I thought she was joking, but it became clear she was not. Another poll worker nearby who heard the conversation prevailed upon her to let me use the bathroom and she very begrudgingly relented. Whoa. Not a good start.

When I came out, she told me never to use it once the polls opened. I was shocked by her rudeness and incivility. Her fellow poll workers told her to stop and said I could use the bathroom as needed during the day as long as I spoke to no voters within 100 feet of the entrance and inside. I reassured them I understood the rule and would abide by it. I had no idea what triggered this poll worker's hostility, but it was clear that she was not pleased with my presence. Cleveland this was not.

My partner from the Obama campaign poll watching committee showed up upon the opening of the polls. She was also a lawyer and due to her Pennsylvania residency, she was permitted inside the polling place to ensure proper poll practices were being followed. We would communicate by phone or she would walk out beyond the 100-foot line to speak to me when taking breaks (designated by cones placed in the parking lot by poll workers).

She was very pleasant and we both understood to be on the lookout for poll workers inadvertently or intentionally requiring voters to produce ID which was not required by the recent court ruling. Of course, the poll workers could ask for ID but if a voter couldn't' produce it this was not a reason to prevent them from casting a ballot. To say it was a stupid and confusing court ruling is an all-time understatement.

I stationed myself inside the church parking lot just on the other side of the 100-foot cone barrier. The lot was small so the vast majority of the voters came on foot and had to walk from the sidewalk through the parking lot to go into the only entrance to the polls. My position was perfect to catch every voter who was going in and out of the polls.

Remember the misinformation campaign that advised the public that ID was required then hidden away from the main message was the sentence it could be asked for but didn't need to be produced? Well that was surely going to be the battle of the day and based on my early morning attack from that one rude poll worker, I was bracing for the worst.

As the day began there was the usual early morning group that came on the way to work. It was a diverse mixture of voters from every race, ethnicity, gender and age. I repeatedly told every voter going in clearly and repeatedly that they were not required to show ID to vote but may be asked by a poll worker to present ID due to a court ruling. I emphasized that whether they had the ID or not they were allowed to vote as long as they were registered in the polling book. Many people looked askance at my advice, but I reassured them it was true (crazy, but true) and if anyone inside denied them their right to vote for failure to produce an ID they should tell me when they come out so I could rectify it for them.

As everyone came out, I asked them if there were any problems and if they got to vote. I know this is sadly predictable but, 100% of the people who had problems in the morning and were denied the right to vote were African-American and Latino. Mere coincidence? Me thinks not.

As I gathered facts from those that were denied the right to vote, every one of them told me the same story. A poll worker found their names as properly registered on the official list then asked to see their ID. When they did not have an ID on them the worker told them they could not vote. I was infuriated. This was the exact opposite of the law and exactly what the lawyers who argued the case on voters' behalf feared would happen due to the judge's confusing ruling.

One by one I wrote down the name of the voter ID case (Applewhite v. Commonwealth) for each voter and told them to go back inside, tell the poll worker that the judge in this case said no voter ID was required and don't leave until they let you vote. I told them that I was not a Pennsylvania lawyer and this was not legal advice but simply public information. I believed that their voting rights were being violated and I advised them that there was a Pennsylvania lawyer inside from the Obama campaign who could tell the poll workers that they were flat out wrong. I told each voter that you registered, you came to vote and no one has the right to deny you from casting your vote.

I knew the kind of person who came early in the morning was a very motivated voter and was sure those voters who were sent away without casting a ballot were not going away so easily. Sure enough, each of those early voters came back to me, told me the poll workers were not happy with them or me, but the Obama campaign lawyer inside of course backed me up and they all got to cast their votes.

As was the procedure, I reported this problem to the Obama campaign voter protection office for follow-up. I understood that they were covering a large city and systemic problems like broken machines and long lines took priority.

The Philadelphia lawyer from the Obama campaign came out to speak to me later in the morning after about 10 of these incidents. All eventually resolved in favor of the voters after I sent them back inside armed with the court decision information so they could fight for their rights with solid documentation.

The lawyer told me that the poll workers were quite disturbed with me for sending voters back in and were concerned that if I kept doing this, I would create long lines when the after-work evening rush came. I literally laughed. They were concerned that my honest and accurate advice about public information is going to get more voters to vote but may make their night longer? Contemptible. Sickening. No better than the Jim Crow South in its disparate impact (that term comes up a lot in this book because bad intent is hard to prove but bad results impacting only two groups – African-Americans and Latinos – is a much different story and is every bit as wrong as intentional discrimination).

Fortunately, some of the poll workers were quite nice and still allowed me to use the restroom during the day. Once or twice the woman who yelled at me at the opening caught my glance with her evil eyes and it was clear to me who was turning away my voters in direct defiance of the court order.

Things did not get better. While the mid-afternoon is traditionally slow, the misinformation campaign inside the church (of all places) did not stop. The stream of voters initially denied their right to vote for not having an ID continued. Of the few dozen people denied their right to vote on the first try, I can only recall one white person. He was a very nice young man, working a minimum wage job and very excited to vote during his work break. I got his vote to be cast when I sent him back in but couldn't help but wonder how this could continue to happen after a few dozen people and the Philadelphia lawyer inside reminded the poll workers of the law and cited the applicable case. That one poll worker, based on a description by voters and the Obama campaign lawyer inside, was intentionally or unintentionally creating a pattern of voter suppression (Intentional or unintentional? You pick.). I will never know her motive for sure, but I know whose votes were being targeted. Maybe 90% were African-Americans, 5% were Latinos and 5% were white. Do we really need to discuss this part of the story anymore?

I repeatedly notified headquarters of this clear violation of the court order and they assured me it would be dealt with through the proper channels as they were putting out fires throughout the city. They called me back a few times so I knew they were on it, but I felt like it was under control to the extent that the voters were consistently winning on the second try.

Why does voting have to be such a difficult thing to do in America? Why can't we just have the easiest system in the world, automatic voter registration (AVR)? AVR means every time there is contact between a citizen over 18 years old with any government agency (Motor Vehicle Agency, Social Service Agency, Veteran's Administration, etc.), the agency must automatically register the voter or re-register with updated information and supply it to the proper election board officials. The voter can opt-out but that would be a very rare occurrence.[56] Secondly, those agencies are required to automatically transfer the voter registration record electronically to election officials so no paper registration is necessary.[57] After Oregon enacted this as the first in the nation, it has become the law in 19 states and D.C. as of April, 2020.[58]

I digress, but such a law would make much of my voter protection work moot since it would avoid so many of the archaic voter registration issues that occur every Election Day throughout America. Remember, voting is the ultimate act of resistance since putting the right candidate in local, state and federal offices results in free and fair elections protected by laws such as Automatic Voter Registration. What are the opponents of AVR afraid of? Everyone voting and everyone's vote being counted? The only people afraid of that are those that can't win elections fair and square by winning the majority of all eligible voters. Now back to Philadelphia.

During an afternoon call, my favorite lady, the yeller and poll worker from hell, came outside to "talk" to me. Well, it was actually to yell at me. She told me I should stop telling voters to come back inside after she told them they can't vote. She advised me that I was going to create long lines during the evening rush if I kept doing this. She even gave me a veiled threat that if I didn't stop, she would take care of me. I said thanks for the advice, but I have no intention of giving out false information and she could make the process a lot easier if she simply followed the law in the first instance instead of making me send back the voters a second time armed with the judge's ruling on not requiring ID to vote.

I thought we left it at a standstill since I was not going to budge one inch. I figured my only defeat was that my bathroom privileges probably ended, but there was a store nearby and a simple purchase would get me access to the facilities. I now thought that all was well. How embarrassingly naive of me.

There were a few more incidents in the mid-afternoon that followed the same pattern. Certain African-American and Latino voters were asked for ID and when they couldn't be produced my "friend" the poll worker sent them packing without allowing them to cast their votes despite being registered. I always caught the voters on the way out and I gave them the case name to show her and gave them a pep talk that their right to vote was sacred and some random poll worker who was not following the law had no right to take away their rights. I guess that second round of them returning to the poll worker with my information wore her down because she kept relenting (except for one voter who gave up after the second try) and let them vote the second time. My only concern was that less aggressive and bashful voters turned away the first time may not have told me about their experiences. Maybe they were late for work. Maybe they were late picking up their children. Very possibly, there were some of those voters who had other commitments and left without voting because of a poll worker's failure to follow the law. Those votes were forever lost and those voters may have been so soured by their awful experiences that they may not come back for years. That's why the struggle never ends. Every voter deserves respect and must walk away knowing their right to vote is precious and should never be suppressed.

I should also mention that my partner inside had been ejected in the afternoon for mirroring my advice with voters inside. She was accused of obstructing the voting process. This, of course, got reported to headquarters and we awaited further resolution of this out of control behavior by the voter suppressing poll worker (Intentionally or unintentionally? Does it really make a difference which if the result is bad?).

Late afternoon arrived and out of nowhere I saw the mean poll worker come out of the entrance with some other poll workers. She was clearly on fire and yelled for me to come over to the group. I was so ready to calmly spit back at her wrath, figuratively of course. She started wailing about me giving wrong advice to voters. She lied about me violating the 100-foot rule. She said I should be arrested. It was almost on cue.

With my back turned to the parking lot entrance, she pointed to me and said "Police. Police. Arrest that man. That's him." As I turned around, I saw two uniformed Philadelphia police officers ride up on bicycles and park right behind me while I was a few feet from the entrance, the area she had called me over to. She started screaming like a lunatic. She told the policemen I was obstructing the voting process. She said I was giving wrong advice to voters. She accused me of riling up voters. She told the officers I was going to create horribly long lines at night by me reckless behavior.

The ranting and raving were completely out of control but as a trial lawyer who cross-examines witnesses, I knew there was an ulterior motive. She was clearly trying to provoke me into a shouting match to show the police I was a hot-headed instigator. This incompetent (that is my kind description in print) started with the wrong person. I let her go on and on as she got louder and more red-faced. I could assess that the police were not pleased with her abusive tone. They had a lot to do on Election Day and this incident must have certainly seemed like the call from hell.

I also realized that the screaming minutes before the police arrived was a set up to provoke me into a loud argument upon arrival by the police. Like I would go for the bait. She had obviously called the police before exiting the building so she was executing on her foolish plan.

While her loud ranting to the police while literally wagging her finger at me continued, I looked over to the two policemen. In a very calm and deliberate voice, I asked them if they would like to hear my version of the day's proceedings. I think they were relieved just to hear the volume come down.

I told the police about the problems with the poll worker giving improper advice to voters and sending them out without being allowed to vote. I told them about my advice to voters and the public information that I gave them about the court order not requiring them to have ID in order to vote. I also told them that the only times I was within the 100-foot line was to use the restroom which I had permission to use. I calmly and politely ended with these words to the two police officers: "If it is a crime in Philadelphia to dispense proper, publicly available advice to voters about an applicable Pennsylvania voting rights court ruling which protects citizens' right to vote, then I should be put in handcuffs and arrested because I am guilty as charged".

The two officers, one white and one African-American, said almost simultaneously in a very calm and polite tone, "Protecting voters? That sounds like a good thing. That's never been a crime in Philadelphia". That stunned the poll worker. She had been exposed for the bully (And voter suppressor? Intentional or unintentional?) that she had been for over eight hours. She could barely talk.

The police made it clear that there were no grounds to charge me with anything other than protecting the right to vote on Election Day. She then raised the issue of me violating the 100-foot rule all day. That was a complete lie and her last, desperate attempt to get rid of me like she did with the lawyer inside who she had expelled earlier. That wasn't going to happen with me. I explained to the police she was dead wrong, but I was willing to propose a compromise. I would agree to leave the parking lot completely despite the fact I was allowed by law to stay in my area of the parking lot since I was posted more than 100 feet from the entrance. I offered to move to the public sidewalk in front of the parking lot entrance. The irascible poll worker told the police that they should order me to stop giving my advice to voters even when I was on the sidewalk. I suggested to the officers that my right to free speech on a public sidewalk could not be abridged by a government employee. They concurred and told her my compromise was eminently fair.

What she didn't realize was that I was selling her air. The area of the public sidewalk where I stationed myself for the rest of the evening was at the only entrance to the parking lot which every car and every pedestrian were required to pass to get to the only doors leading to the polling place. I did not give away my ability to speak to every voter going in and out of the poll. I gave away nothing and got everything. The poll worker stormed away in defeat (though she foolishly thought she got a partial victory by banishing me to the sidewalk), not realizing that my compromise would not stop me from approaching every voter and sending back voters if she wrongfully denied them from voting for not having ID. The two officers were very reasonable and professional. Before leaving, they even thanked me for coming all the way down to Philadelphia at my expense and volunteering my time and skills to protect voters. They got it. She didn't and probably never will.

I called into headquarters with my police incident story and they listened with disbelief. I quoted all of the participants in the verbal melee to the intake person at headquarters. She literally started clapping on the phone. Someone else got on the phone and also excitedly congratulated me. I now had some real interest from headquarters about what was going on and they said a team would be dispatched to have a little talk with the troublemaker poll worker during the expectedly busy after-work shift.

My strategy worked like a charm. The evening rush started and I spoke to every single voter about the ID problem as they entered and exited since they had no choice but to pass me where I was stationed on the sidewalk. I had very few incidents at night of poll workers turning away my voters on the ID issue after the police incident. The team also showed up from headquarters during the after-work shift and had a talk with the poll worker which kept the momentum going for no ID problems the rest of the night.

When the team showed up it turned into a very gratifying moment. They told me I was the talk of the local headquarters. I was known as the guy willing to be arrested in the name of voting rights. They treated me like royalty. They invited me to the presumed victory party and said there were a lot of people back at headquarters who were impressed that I put myself in danger of arrest in the name of fighting voter suppression. I was really honored by their kind words. It made me feel like I really accomplished some good things in the name of free and fair elections.

The rest of the evening was a success. As much as I would have loved to meet the rest of the voting rights crew at the party, the past week coupled with this extraordinary day left me completely exhausted. I drove straight back to my hotel to have a nice meal in my room while watching the election returns.

What a gratifying day to be able to help so many voters be able to cast their ballots when they were initially turned away in defiance of the court order. I could not have written a better script. Admittedly, the trial lawyer part of me reveled in the pugnacious assault perpetrated upon me by that annoying (I am trying hard to be nice in print) poll worker. I loved standing up to her multiple times that day. I basked in the confrontation of good versus evil. I was proud to tell the police I was guilty of being a voter protection advocate. I thoroughly enjoyed the day and most of all my voters triumphed. It made a real difference for them to have someone advise them, support them, arm them with the facts and motivate them to jump back into the polling place after they were denied the right to vote. It doesn't get better than that for me on Election Day. That was a resounding victory even before the election results were in.

I plopped down to watch the results on TV as my feet told me it was time to lie down. While it was a little closer in 2012 than in 2008, America rewarded President Obama with the re-election that he deserved. He avoided a national economic depression, he signed the most sweeping health care act (the Affordable Care Act now known as "Obamacare") in our nation's history and he stopped a seemingly endless presence of U.S. troops in Iraq – a war that Bush lied us into with false information. This was another good night for the American electorate.

His victory speech that evening would be prophetic since he spoke of what really makes America great years before the red hats with their hollow slogan, implying a return to a past of injustice and inequality, came into our public consciousness:

"This country has more wealth than any nation, but that's not what makes us rich. We have the most powerful military in history, but that's not what makes us strong. Our universities, our culture are all the envy of the world, but that's not what keeps the world coming to our shores. What makes America exceptional are the bonds that hold together the most diverse nation on Earth, the belief that our destiny is shared — (cheers, applause) — that this country only works when we accept certain obligations to one another and to future generations, so that the freedom which so many Americans have fought for and died for come with responsibilities as well as rights, and among those are love and charity and duty and patriotism. That's what makes America great."[59]

In what has now become a tradition, my wife and I made plans for the Inauguration. It would be another inspiring event as well as a lovely visit to D.C. for a longer stay than in 2009. The 2013 visit is best summed up in another email that I shared with my friends upon our return:

"Dear Friends:

Florence and I just returned from a remarkable experience in Washington, D.C. as witnesses to the second Inaugural Address of President Obama.

We stood on the National Mall from 5:25 A.M. with hundreds of thousands of our fellow Americans (in the non-ticketed public area) to reaffirm our faith in this centuries old form of government known as American democracy.

We arrived in Washington on Saturday with renewed hope and optimism in President Obama's second term leadership and we left on Tuesday with certitude that the man who took the oath of office is a historic figure who deeply understands our past, instinctively knows the path to a better present and clearly envisions a glorious American future built upon our founding principles of equality, freedom and opportunity for all Americans.

We stood for eight hours to support our democracy and our elected leader among a mass of humanity representing every race, ethnicity, gender, sexual orientation and age group. This experience crystallized the American experience for me once again. Our American greatness comes from both our diversity and our commonality. Our greatness comes from both our shared experiences and our different experiences that we share with each other. Our greatness comes from both our openness to new ideas, new immigrants and new possibilities and our resolve to turn ideas into action.

The President reminded us all that the Preamble to the United States Constitution begins with "We the People". **We the People** have always been the force behind noble and righteous ideals. **We the People** are the force for good, the force for equality and the force for justice for all. **We the People** are the masters of our nation's fate. **We the People** rose up against tyranny at our birth and must forever fight to preserve our democracy against those who threaten it with their small minds, small hearts and small visions.

While substantive debate in our democracy is always healthy, there are those among us in this nation who have opposed President Obama for four years for reasons that bring shame to our republic. Opposition based on restriction of rights for women, gays and immigrants is un-American. Opposition based on the creation of pernicious obstacles to voting rights for African-Americans and Latinos is un-American. Opposition based on the denial of science to stop progress in the area of climate change for future generations is un-American.

Florence and I were humbled by the outpouring of true patriotism and national pride in that wonderful crowd composed of the American mosaic on Monday. We were emotionally and intellectually moved by the depth of President Obama's address especially in the majestic setting of the U.S. Capitol and the Washington Monument embracing us on opposite ends of the National Mall.

On Tuesday, we were honored to visit memorials built in honor of Dr. Martin Luther King, Jr. and Franklin Delano Roosevelt along the Tidal Basin below the National Mall. The words inscribed at those memorials were reminders that America has a rich history of great leaders who thought big, who thought deeply, who thought for their day and who thought for future days for generations to come.

When we looked out on the basin from the FDR Memorial we saw on one end the Jefferson Memorial and on the other end the Martin Luther King, Jr. Memorial. The historical bridge from Thomas Jefferson, a slaveholder who wrote of future equality, to Dr. King, a descendent from slaves who fought and died for equality, was built by **We the People**. Our nation's stated ideals of equality have progressed through the centuries, often at a glacial pace, but always moving forward.

Dr. King did not live to see his dream, our dream, come to fruition. We in 2013 have not seen his dream, our dream, become a reality for all. As dedicated Americans, however, **We the People** continue to work to make equality a societal given and not a societal goal.

As President Obama reminded us on Monday, our Declaration of Independence stated, "We hold these truths to be self-evident, that all men are created equal." He also delivered a powerful reminder: "For history tells us that while these truths are self-evident, they've never been self-executing."

However you choose to strengthen our democracy - through volunteering for an organization in your community, visiting an elderly shut-in neighbor or joining Organizing for Action at **www.barackobama.com** - the time to do it is now.

We will not be derailed by the extremists in our nation who say no to environmental progress, who say no to civil rights for all, who say no to equality of opportunity, who say no to voting rights for all, who say no to stopping the gun madness.

Four years ago, we declared for all the world to hear, YES WE CAN. We must now do as we said. YES, WE WILL.

Sincerely,
Richard C. Bell"

CHAPTER SEVEN

Just a Little Bit

While 2014 saw a successful return to my court hearing advocacy in Bergen County, New Jersey, it was 2013 that sticks out in my mind from that timeframe. In 2013, I was bestowed a great honor by my college mentor Dr. Raymond Gavins. He invited me back to Duke University to speak at his seminar entitled, "Post-Civil Rights America, the Search for Social Justice."

My wife Florence and I flew down for a long weekend since it was also my every 5-year college reunion which I attended religiously ever since my graduation. I have very fond memories of my undergraduate years as a history major at Duke. I had the privilege of studying under Dr. Gavins in his African-American History courses. As I described in the introduction, Dr. Gavins is a giant in his field as well as one of the finest human beings I have ever had the honor of knowing. He was taken from us very suddenly and much too soon in 2016 while still teaching at Duke.

We had been back in touch since 2008 after many years. We rekindled an important relationship in my life since he inspired so much of my world view about voting rights, racial injustice and a path toward true equality for all Americans. He was not just an esteemed scholar, but a hero to me. He personified the spirit of justice that I try to live up to every day in my law practice, voter protection work and life in general. I wish every reader got to know him like me and thousands of his Duke students over 40 plus years as one of the most important and quietly inspirational professors who ever taught on that lovely campus. Please re-read my Acknowledgment about him. He deserves to be remembered with great fondness and introduced to those of you who will only know him from this book.

When Dr. Gavins invited me, he asked if I could speak to his class about my voting rights work. He thought it would give his students some perspective on what can be done tangibly to promote social justice. I took my responsibility very seriously. I recalled my years sitting in Dr. Gavins' classroom and absorbing so many lessons that lasted me a lifetime. I thought long and hard how to keep the students' interest and impact them with a message that they could actually use one day.

Dr. Gavins in his usual genteel manner made some kind introductory remarks before the small number of students in his seminar. It was a class that was scheduled for over an hour so he gave me 15 minutes to present my "lecture". I felt this was a prime opportunity to pass on what Dr. Gavins had passed onto me many decades before – know the past so you can make a difference in the future in the name of those who sacrificed in the struggle for social justice.

I entitled my talk, "Just a Little Bit". I told the students that their wonderful professor had imparted in me his wisdom and historical knowledge of the struggle for equality in America. His guidance at my young age left me with the duty to do my small part over the years to move the needle of social justice forward, if just a little bit. I told them how he opened my eyes to look at history from the perspective of the oppressed who didn't get the chance to write the first version of history.

They learned how Dr. Gavins had opened my mind and heart in a transformational way at an impressionable time in my life. I reminded them that Dr. Martin Luther King in 1965 profoundly emphasized to us all that **"Voting is the foundation stone for political action."**[60]

I then told them of my voting rights experiences that I now recounted to you in this book. They learned about the elderly woman from Mississippi who taught me the meaning of fighting for voting rights in Cleveland in 2004; the young woman who fought valiantly in 2008 in that New Jersey courtroom to preserve her right to vote in the face of public humiliation in a courtroom (as I perceived it); and the necessity of me facing down a vile poll worker who tried to get me arrested for informing voters of their rights in Philadelphia in 2012. After each story, I reminded them that I helped move the needle of social justice forward, if just a little bit.

I told the students, all very bright and engaged, that my stories were to remind them that social justice is not only about famous marches and oft-quoted leaders celebrated in history. Its deepest roots are in ordinary citizens fighting to protect the rights of their fellow ordinary citizens on an individual scale by moving the needle of social justice forward, even if just a little bit.

I told them that we cannot all be the voice and face of the Civil Rights Movement like Dr. King; or become the chairperson of the Civil Rights Commission like Dr. Mary Frances Berry (one of Dr. Gavins' favorite mentions in my college classes with him in the 70's); or be the quiet hero and trailblazer who becomes the first African-American to receive a Ph.D. from the University of Virginia Graduate School of Arts and Sciences in 1970 and then goes on to devote a lifetime to opening the minds and hearts of thousands of Duke students, inspiring them to do their part to right the wrongs of social injustice. That last one was obviously about Dr. Gavins who never told me that story but couldn't hide it from Mr. Google. He was such a humble man that he blushed in the back of the classroom as I looked at him while saying it. I did get him to break into an embarrassed little smile of acknowledgment.

I told these future leaders that wherever their career paths took them, they all had the ability and the obligation to apply their skills, hearts and minds to move the needle of social justice forward, if just a little bit. They were of a generation where splash, celebrity and self-promotion often overwhelmed quiet acts of the modern heroes of social justice. They needed to hear that in our small deeds we honor heroes like Dr. Gavins who have moved the needle of social justice forward much more than a little bit without fanfare, public adulation or television cameras.

They needed to be told directly from someone like me who sat in their seats decades ago that whether they became historians or hedge fund managers, attorneys or artists, physicists or financial analysts the duty is the same. The duty is to use their power to affect social change, if only a little bit. That may mean being a voting rights advocate. It may mean petitioning and marching for racial justice, gay rights and equality for the disabled in their home states. It may simply be getting 3 friends previously unregistered to get registered and vote in the next election.

I told them what I believe to my very core and what Dr. Gavins always encouraged in the classroom through readings and discussions about historical figures both famous and not so famous. Just do your good deeds with the knowledge that every social justice movement begins with small but passionate acts of mostly anonymous individuals who move the needle of social justice forward, if just a little bit.

We all need to live the words that Dr. King uttered to an audience in Washington, D.C. in 1959, **"Make a career of humanity, commit yourself to the noble struggle for equal rights, you will make a greater person of yourself, a greater nation of your country, and a finer world to live in"**.[61]

The students seemed to be interested in my words. As I was about to sit down, Dr. Gavins told me to remain standing for the rest of the seminar to conduct a Q&A with the students. As a trial lawyer who was passionate about social justice this was like a dream. The students were highly informed and provocative in a way that young, curious minds should be. What a delightful surprise to get to speak for the whole class time.

One student in particular stood out for his approach to his inquiry. He referred to the Supreme Court case which was currently pending at that time in April 2013. The Voting Rights Act of 1965 was being challenged in a case named Shelby County, Alabama v. Holder, Attorney General, et al.[62] The constitutionality of part of the historic Voting Rights Act was being put to a historic test. He was a bit smug (as I probably was at his age when I too thought I was so smart before growing up and realizing that true knowledge is knowing you don't really know so much) in posing his question as why the court even took on such a case when it was so obvious that the whole Voting Rights Act would be upheld since voter suppression and voting discrimination against people of color was still prevalent as evidenced by so many documented reports as well as the few stories I told them today.

I was taken aback by his confidence that upholding the act was a done deal. I told him as a lawyer I had no confidence that the current Supreme Court would do the right thing. I read Bush v. Gore and other Supreme Court decisions with horror and questioned the intellectual honesty of the conservative majority. I reiterated that I would never predict that the Voting Rights Act would be upheld as constitutional by the five justices necessary to form a majority. I warned him to be concerned that a terrible decision could come down that would rip a hole the size of New York into voting rights in America. He looked at me like I had three heads and he politely disagreed.

I wish I could have seen his expression when two months later the court ruled 5-4 that Section 4 of the 1965 Voting Rights Act was unconstitutional.[63] Section 4 was a vital part of the act because it required nine states (mostly in the South) to get pre-clearance from a federal court or the U.S. Justice Department before changing any voting laws to prevent laws that would create the very racial discrimination that the original act intended to make unlawful.[64]

As I feared, the Roberts Court for reasons that make no rational sense to me in essence invited those southern states to enact laws that have disparate impact on racial minorities without the safeguard of pre-clearance. After the fact court challenges are so much more difficult than pre-clearance actions. Any sitting justice should have known that fact. The Chief Justice essentially concluded that the 1965 era of racial discrimination in voting was over to which dissenting Justice Ginsberg responded that racial discrimination in voting is a continuum, not a relic of the past, "The great man who led the march from Selma to Montgomery and there called for the passage of the Voting Rights Act foresaw progress, even in Alabama . . . 'The arc of the moral universe is long' he said, but 'it bends toward justice', if there is a steadfast commitment to see the task through to completion."[65]

This dangerous action by the Supreme Court less than 6 months after President Obama's second term began was an ominous sign of more bad things to come for voting rights in America. Predictably, hours after the June 2013 ruling Texas declared it would push to enforce a voter ID requirement and Mississippi and Alabama, which had been awaiting federal approval of their voter ID laws under Section 4 of the Voting Rights Act, were now ready to enforce the law with those constraints now lifted by the new Supreme Court ruling.[66]

As time would pass, the most strict voter ID laws became a great tool for voter suppression by having disparate impact on turnout of African-Americans, Latinos and mixed-race Americans to the detriment of Democratic candidates (no surprise there).[67] As time went on, of course, this obstacle was matched with other effective voter suppression laws such as "shortened early voting periods, repeal of same day voter registration, reduced polling hours, a decrease in polling locations, and increased restrictions on voting by felons . . ."[68] The argument has always been that "the correct ID can require money and transportation to a state's Department of Motor Vehicles branch or local government office, resources some voters may not have".[69] This explains why the stricter the ID requirement, the more potential there is for voter suppression which disproportionately affects minority communities.[70]

In 2012 there were 4 states that required photo ID for voters to cast their ballots and by 2016 that rose to 32 states with 7 states having the strictest laws that require voters without the proper ID on Election Day to cast a "provisional ballot", which means that ballot will not be counted unless they produce the required ID within a short time after Election Day.[71] Provisional ballots are known as the wasteland of ballots because they often require a voter to take an additional action after Election Day (such as production of an ID); this results in many provisional ballots not being counted with a great variance from state to state (from over 85% counted in California to a low of 29% counted in Texas in 2008).[72]

Whichever side of the partisan divide you may fall on, does anyone seriously want to argue that making voting fast, easy and fair is ever wrong? Please don't even think about the false narrative that the above obstacles to voting are enacted to prevent widespread voter fraud. That conspiracy theory has been debunked every time it rears its false, ugly head since at most there is .0025% fraudulent casting of ballots which is beyond statistically insignificant.[73] We need to stop dignifying this empirically baseless argument with any semblance of a debate.[74] There is no debate.[75] This is clearly a straw man argument raised by the voter suppression brigade. Hello again, Donald.

CHAPTER EIGHT

Florida 2016:

The Voting Rights Nightmare that Never Seems to End

As the 2016 presidential election campaign got into gear early in 2015, many people felt it would be a Bush-Clinton rematch with Jeb and Hillary leading the major party tickets. What seemed at the time to be a ridiculous distraction was the announced candidacy of Donald Trump who was known to many of us in the New York City area as a publicity hungry, race-baiting, failed businessman who literally questioned President Obama's American citizenship. It was rather embarrassing that the media spotlight shined on New York City as he made that pompous ride down (the direction in which he has precipitously taken the country) the Trump Tower escalator to deliver those infamous, hateful words,

"When Mexico sends its people, they're not sending their best, they're sending people that have lots of problems and they're bringing those problems with us [sic]. They're bringing drugs, they're bringing crime, they're rapists. And some, I assume, are good people".[76]

As the months waned on, what once seemed unfathomable became possible, probable then sadly real. Trump actually became the standard bearer of the Republicans in spite of or because of his xenophobia, racism, misogyny and other despicable traits. While many were very disappointed that a portion of the voters actually supported his unprecedented candidacy of hate (I don't consider George Wallace as precedent since he was not a major party candidate), surely Hillary would trounce him in the election.

When deciding where I would do my voter protection work in 2016, I knew I wanted to be in a hot spot where Hillary needed me. It became clear Florida was going to be its usual closely contested race. Due to its large number of electoral votes, 29, and its sordid election history it would be a great place for me to protect the vote and elect our first female president. Famous last words.

As the weeks leading up to Election Day passed, there was an unnerving sense that it may no longer be an expected landslide for Hillary. She would win, of course, but it might end up a lot closer as indicated by the volatile polls which seemed to show a significant narrowing of the gap.

My assignment was in Broward County, Florida which is the home of Fort Lauderdale. It is a Democratic stronghold which means it was fertile ground for voter suppression of the Democratic base of African-American and Latino voters in South Florida. It took me 16 years after the 2000 election debacle, but I was finally going to get to do voter protection work in America's largest battleground state. Be careful what you wish for.

For those who have been to Florida, you know it's a very mixed bag. There is a combination of traditional Southerners, lots of transplanted New Yorkers and residents from other Northern states and a very diverse cultural mix from around the world. There is no one Florida. There is no one defined culture. There is no single overriding theme to the state like you find elsewhere. Its large transient population and enormous tourist presence make it very hard to define what is the real Florida. I would soon find out about the real Florida as an Election Day nightmare unfolded.

My work in Cleveland, Philadelphia and New Jersey all required me to study and become proficient in the state voter laws and expected Election Day issues in each venue. Florida was a whole other story. There was a video online presentation in addition to the written materials provided by the Florida Democratic election protection team. That sounded normal. What came next was bizarre for someone who works in Manhattan and grew up very close to America's largest city.

In other cities, the discussion about potential problems centered around voter ID, moves by a voter within the state or inordinately long lines. In Florida, the hypothetical on the training video that floored me went something like this, "A man in military fatigues is pacing the sidewalk outside the 100-foot area of a polling place in an African-American neighborhood carrying an assault weapon and telling people he is exercising his 1st and 2nd Amendment rights to make sure no one tries to steal the election for Hillary". Stop. Did the video and materials say someone was carrying an assault weapon? I literally thought that was a poor taste joke until the instructor calmly advised the online out-of-state lawyers that this is a possible scenario on Election Day in Florida. In Philadelphia poll workers call the police on me and in Florida I should need to worry about a guy in fatigues with an assault rifle? Whoa. Welcome to Florida.

The prospect of even the chance of a Trump presidency brought volunteer lawyers to Florida from coast to coast in 2016. I met a very informed and interesting group of lawyers from Florida, Washington, New Jersey and many other states. All of them shared my reaction to the gun-toting training course example and hoped it would remain a hypothetical on Election Day.

I arrived in Fort Lauderdale on the Friday night before Election Day since Fort Lauderdale had early voting at designated polls on Saturday and Sunday before the election. Just as in the other cities I had worked in, each out-of-state lawyer was paired with a Florida lawyer since she could be inside the polls to observe as a resident and I could be outside to communicate directly with the voters (she could only speak to the poll workers, not the voters directly). I hit pay dirt when I was paired with "Jane" on Saturday at a large polling place in a predominately African-American neighborhood in Broward County.[77]

Jane is an extremely intelligent lawyer with the aggressive instincts of someone who grew up in the New York City area (she did). She is very personable, but equally tough. She is also very experienced at voter protection. She was a perfect match for me.

In the materials, I learned that Florida by 2016 had a peculiar (poor choice of words since everything about Florida elections is peculiar) law regarding voting of ex-felons. Ex-felons were originally stripped of their rights to vote during 19th century Reconstruction and the Jim Crow era well into the 20th century with obvious racist roots.[78] In the 2000's Florida had a very severe and unforgiving law originally enacted after the Civil War that banned ex-felons from voting which affected well over a million people, disproportionately African-American.[79] Governor Charlie Crist (a Republican, Independent and Democrat in his career) in 2007 made a fundamental change in voting rights by making it very simple for ex-felons to get their voting rights restored with a streamlined process, after finishing their sentences and probation.[80] Unfortunately, in 2011 Republican Governor Rick Scott changed the rules making the backlog extraordinary and the process very cumbersome.[81] A later study showed that under Governor Scott the voting rights of twice as many white former felons were restored as compared to black former felons.[82] Surprise. Surprise. You think that helped him in his subsequent campaign for senator? Just asking. This Florida history lesson would become valuable as my voter protection dive into Florida elections began.

Day one in Florida. My usual suit and tie were fine in my northeast appearances, but it was a little less comfortable in the hot South Florida sun in November. It was not required attire but I was always taught to look like a lawyer in performing my job so I clung to my principles to look the role that I loved. The afternoon started off with a good flow of early voters hoping to avoid the long lines on Tuesday. Always an excellent voting strategy.

Armed with my tablet, phone and incident reporting app, I was confronted with a strange issue early on. An ex-felon said he was told he could not vote because his voting rights were not restored. He recalled that during the Governor Crist years he had his rights restored but the poll worker could not find his "rights restored" data in the county voting records. He swore that he had been allowed to register to vote but could not find proof of same.

At first, we thought this was an isolated incident of a voter who simply didn't remember correctly about his voter restoration and possibly had not received final notification of restoration due to the long wait imposed by the Governor Scott order.[83] Then the issue exploded. The same scenario happened for many dozens of voters and all of them had the same recollection. Of course, the polling place was correctly turning the voters away since they were not in the registration system. However, it was more than coincidental that so many voters had the same story. Unfortunately, there was nothing we could do for them because none of them had a certificate of restoration to go along with a prior voter registration. This was such a strange situation since in 12 years of doing voter protection I never encountered this issue. Florida was obviously a vestige of the old South with this antiquated post-Civil War law that obviously grew from an intent to disenfranchise former slaves.[84] It was heart-breaking to see so many African-Americans and Latinos show up excited to vote after having paid their debt to society only to be sent away from the polls because there was either a glitch in the registration system or something much worse. I'll never know the true reason why so many ex-felons whose voting rights may have been restored did not make it onto the voter registration rolls. I do know that the disappointment each and every voter expressed to me was haunting.

Fast forward for some perspective. While the voters in Florida passed a felon re-enfranchisement referendum on Election Day 2018, the Republican legislature and Governor DeSantis (the all-time Trump sycophant) passed a law adding poll tax-like restrictions such as requiring payment of

fines, fees and restitution before becoming re-enfranchised.
[85] While a federal trial level court called the requirements
an unconstitutional voting tax, of course the 11th Circuit
Appeals court so far has blocked the order preventing hundreds of thousands of ex-felons from registering to vote in
the 2020 elections.[86] The U.S. Supreme Court very recently
let the appeals court decision stand as 1.4 million ex-felons
await a final decision by the lower federal courts.[87] Stay
tuned, this is Florida so all bets are off until Election Day
2020 actually arrives. Hopefully, but not likely, the final
2020 court ruling will allow the people's will in 2018 to be
followed and permit more than 1 million ex-felons to get an
opportunity to vote as all Americans should. Then again,
this is Florida so who knows.

With those dozens of ex-felons denied their right to vote
that day, Jane and I along with the other Democratic lawyers were left very frustrated without a remedy. We spoke
to headquarters but no good answer was proffered. Florida
elections, never a dull moment.

The upside was that many voters with minor registration
issues were helped by a group of volunteer lawyers. There was
lots of excitement outside the polls with competing electioneering by representatives from various local candidates. It was
a very spirited bunch who kept the afternoon and evening
lively. On another level the day was disappointing due to the
revelation of the ex-felon issue that made me feel like I was
in the Jim Crow South (the poll workers were following the

rules properly but the whole racist concept of this ex-felon law, its implementation and its execution was disheartening).

One of the election campaigners outside the polling place was a very lively man whose zeal was non-stop. He went from afternoon to evening at a record pace giving out flyers for his candidate and talking up a storm on her behalf. He also seemed to know everybody. When the polls closed, he told Jane and I and a few others that his friend owned a barbeque place nearby with outstanding food. He told us to meet him there and he would introduce us to his friend the proprietor.

About a mile away from the place I could see from my car smoke billowing in what seemed like a desolate abandoned lot. As I approached, I saw what looked like a makeshift barbeque pit, a converted truck/kitchen and a bunch of wooden tables and chairs occupied by a big crowd. Jane, her husband, another lawyer and me were the only white people in the crowd and our friend and the proprietor treated us with exuberant warmth and hospitality. The owner showered us with free appetizers while our orders were being prepared and he even set up a special table for us among the large gathering of customers. It was a festive atmosphere. Then came the food. Wow. Literally finger-licking good. The ribs were superb, the mac and cheese was delicious and the sweet potato pie was out of this world. The patrons, our friend from the polls and the owner could not have been more hospitable. What a nice way to cap off the day.

It was a delightful dinner that helped cloud the memory of a frustrating day of watching systemic voter suppression of African-American and Latino ex-felons whether intended or unintended by the State of Florida. I will never understand the point of racism and fear of other. All it does is deny people the chance to participate in the fullness of life and the greatness of diversity. Shared cultures and traditions are the essence of appreciating our diverse backgrounds. It's awful enough that so many people self-segregate and miss out on the joy of celebrating our common humanity without artificial barriers. Of course, I get to see when those obstructions become legal barriers and deny people the right to vote in a clearly discriminatory fashion. Well, at least Hillary was promoting the "Stronger Together" theme while her unworthy opponent was fanning the flames of hate. No one knew on Saturday that hate would triumph on Tuesday.

Sunday was a repeat of Saturday with the ex-felon issues. Sadly, this was the theme at my polling place. Unfortunately, we were powerless to change the results since whatever caused those ex-felons not to be in the registration books as "restored" could not be changed by Election Day.

We helped as many voters as we could with some registration issues that could be fixed. The simple issue that frequently arose was people who were Florida residents and properly registered had moved to the polling precinct recently but were registered at their old addresses. The law allowed them to vote at the new precinct where they resided at as long as they would sign an affidavit of new address at the new polling place. There were no problems doing this at the polling site on Saturday and Sunday. I cannot say with certainty, but the well-trained poll workers (predominantly African-American) in this heavily African-American polling place followed the law to a T and except for the ex-felon issues which they had no control over, the 2 days there were otherwise smooth.

Our friend who recommended the barbeque place on Saturday was back on Sunday too. This time he recommended a peach cobbler that was being sold by a woman from her car in the parking lot. The man was an obvious foodie so I bought 2, 1 for me and 1 for Jane. It was otherworldly. He had a quite the discerning palate.

When the polls opened that Sunday, I experienced my first "souls to the polls" march. It was an African-American tradition there for groups of voters to go directly from church to the polls on Sunday. The group of a few hundred came from the large parking lot led by music and fanfare. It was wonderful to see people so excited about voting. They were the reason I was doing this volunteer work. They understood the tragic history of bloodshed and sacrifice that went into the right to vote for African-Americans. They are from the South and understood that the struggle never ends. It rarely gets easier. It is never over. It was very inspiring.

On Monday I worked with a lawyer from Seattle canvassing in a Broward County community to encourage people to vote on Tuesday since there was no early voting in Florida on Monday. I was a bit concerned by the utter lack of voting enthusiasm I felt as we walked the neighborhood. The Florida polls had Hillary leading slightly and the national polls had narrowed but almost every prognostication had Hillary pegged to be our next President. I was cautiously optimistic but really had no fear that someone as intellectually bankrupt, hateful and totally incompetent as Trump could actually win on Tuesday. That reality truly did not cross my mind. For that matter, I was probably joined by the vast majority of Americans in my thinking on Monday.

I was assigned to be with my partner Jane on Election Day. We had really bonded as a team and I was grateful to be back with her for showtime. We were assigned to a Fort Lauderdale suburb where trouble was anticipated since there was a large contingency of Trump supporters mixing with a minority of African-American and Latino voters. Certainly, that seemed like a formula for trouble. Frankly, I would be happy just to avoid that hypothetical guy in fatigues with the automatic weapon.

I did my scouting drive and timed out the trip from my Fort Lauderdale hotel to the polling place. It was some kind of tennis club/private recreational facility. It seemed fairly upscale and felt very, how should I say, very "un-inclusively" white. There, I said it.

My extremely early arrival routine got me there about 90 minutes before the 7:00 AM opening time which is always my quiet time to study my notes, check my supplies (dozens of bottles of water and energy bars for thirsty and hungry voters if a line forms at some point) and test my phone, tablet and mophies (I fully endorse them as great portable phone chargers.) When I saw the poll workers arriving, I got a pretty chilly greeting but I just kept smiling and reassuring the outside poll worker I understood the 100-foot rule and would not be of any bother during the day (no problem with restroom clearance so that was a better start than Philadelphia). She was stern and humorless but not rude.

Jane arrived to do the inside work and we had received a written ruling that our texting was totally acceptable under the election procedures for the county. As Jane went inside, two campaign representatives arrived to pass out pamphlets for their candidates on the walkway near me. The guy with the MAGA hat looked like he was out of a cartoon with his Trump buttons and lots of Trump red clothing. The woman next to him was campaigning for a local Republican candidate but had her array of Trump buttons as well. My suit and tie, New Jersey accent and voter protection sign and button clued them in as to where I stood on the election. I went out of my way to engage them politely and with humor. They weren't exactly laugh-a-minute people but there was no outward hostility. I offered them water and energy bars to make sure they knew I only expected we would all do our jobs fairly and respectfully. The automatic weapon hypothetical may have also been in the back of the head.

At no point were they rude to me or any way obstructive to voters. The only comments they made that I do recall was when they set themselves up a good distance from me later in the morning which I thought was their attempt to get out of the hot South Florida sun. I think they assumed they were set up too far away from me to hear their conversation but they were wrong. I clenched my teeth as they spoke in hush voices to each other making not so veiled racist and antisemitic statements about Hillary supporters. It was not a time to engage these haters. It was a time to focus on my job to beat them at the polls by making sure that the people they hated were able to exercise their right to vote. That would turn out to be quite a challenge.

While Saturday and Sunday started with the ex-felon issue, it did not arise at all during Election Day at my polling place. However, an early issue arose when one African-American voter said to me outside that he was a registered Florida voter but had recently moved to this precinct and had not changed his address for voter registration purposes. I told him that was not a problem as long as he was a registered voter at the old address and had a valid photo ID with a signature (of course Florida was an ID state) he could vote on the machine at the precinct by signing an affidavit confirming his new address. I texted Jane to tell her he was coming in with the issue. The Florida law was crystal clear so this obviously wouldn't be a problem. I really didn't get Florida yet.

The gentleman goes in and he is there for quite a long time yet the polling place is fairly empty at this early hour. I get a frantic text from Jane that the polling clerk will not let the man fill out an affidavit of address change, will not let him vote on the machine and will not even let him fill out a provisional ballot (he was absolutely entitled under the law to vote on the machine). When he came out the man was livid. I told him he was a victim of blatant voter suppression and I took down his name, address and phone number to file a report with headquarters to resolve the issue. I told him to wait while I spoke to headquarters and I was advised to send him back in, have Jane read the applicable statute to the poll clerk and demand that the man be allowed to vote. The voter dutifully followed everything I told him, Jane texted me that she followed the instructions and the poll clerk still refused to let him vote. When the man came out again, he was rightfully on fire. I spoke to headquarters again in his presence and advised him he would be contacted later in the day by headquarters after they would try to get the Supervisor of Elections of Broward County to intervene and have him come back to vote. The man was exasperated. I was shocked by the clerk's blatant disregard for the law. And Jane, beside herself, came outside in a fury and said "welcome to elections in Florida".

Jane and I both made multiple calls back to headquarters and told them it was urgent for someone from the office of the Supervisor of Elections to come down to the polling place and straighten this out before it became an all-day pattern and practice. They assured me they were working on it.

Not fast enough apparently. The same pattern played out a second time, and a third time, and a fourth time with the same clerk and African-American voters. Jane raised hell inside with the clerk and I literally screamed on the phone at the lawyer at headquarters that overt, intentional and despicable racism and voter suppression was going on at this fancy tennis club with impunity and someone needed to go to court to get an injunction immediately. I was assured this would reach the highest levels of the campaign and be resolved. I am not afraid to say that the clerk was no better than the Jim Crow poll workers of yesteryear in the disparate impact his conduct had upon African-American voters in Democratic Broward County (whether intentional or unintentional). It must have felt like this in 1950's Mississippi (but a whole lot worse). Was it intentional racism? Was it disparate impact without intention? Did it really matter which it was since African-American voters were being suppressed whatever the real motive of the poll worker was? It was stomach-churning to watch this go on without consequences. I decided Florida elections are in a class by themselves (I haven't done voter protection in Georgia so I really should reserve judgment.).

In fairness to the lawyers at headquarters, they took our reports very seriously (Jane and I must have each called every 10 minutes until we got a satisfactory answer) and the alert was moving up the chain of command fairly rapidly (Florida rapidly is not New Jersey or New York rapidly of course).

After about half a dozen similar incidents all involving African-American voters, the office of the Supervisor of Elections directly contacted the clerk and told him to knock it off or else (I had no idea what "else" meant in Florida). He was told if those specific voters came back (they were called and told to do so) they were to be escorted back in to vote on the machine (A few fortunately did come back and cast their votes so that was a partial triumph.).

As a student of history, I could only imagine with horror how it was (and maybe is) in small towns of yesteryear (and very possibly today) where no one comes to protect voters and the local authorities are part of the suppression machine. The bigger problem was this was a metropolitan area in a populous Democratic county in South Florida and it was happening in front of me in 2016. I could only imagine what really went on in Florida during the 2000 election.

To the credit of the election supervisor's office, the in-competent (or malicious) poll clerk started to obey the law when African-American voters came in with the same issue in the afternoon and allowed them to vote. That only lasted a few hours before he went back to his wicked ways. Jane and I went ballistic and the volume of our screams to head-quarters did not require the use of our phones. The same pattern, the same targeting of African-Americans, the same resolution within an hour or so with the election supervisor's office reprimand of him again, but not removal of him from the polling place (that would have been the right sanction). Probably another dozen or so people were affected (some did come back later thankfully and got to cast their votes). In an arrogant display of defiance, he had returned to his unlawful behavior when he apparently thought he could get away with it again since the supervisor's office had a lot of other fires to put out. By day's end, the poll worker had targeted (intentionally or unintentionally?) a few Latino voters as well on the same issue. Deplorable.

As much as Jane and I badgered headquarters all day and got the two reprimands that changed his behavior in spurts, I felt helpless at times because a number of voters were turned away and never came back. They were likely denied the right to vote because of the color of their skin in 2016 and that is forever unforgivable in our democracy.

As awful as this clerk was (at best he didn't know the law, at worst he knew the law and didn't care), we warned headquarters that they should inquire throughout the state if this pattern of voter suppression on the issue of address change was prevalent in other parts of Florida. The clerk kept using the excuse that he was following the law as he understood it (he was either a liar or an idiot, but either way he was having a bad disparate impact upon black and brown voters). I could only imagine how often this went on elsewhere.

My hunch about a pattern and practice was confirmed by an online article I read that evening that there were reports in

Miami-Dade and Palm Beach counties of clerks "mistaken-ly" (yeah, right) preventing voters from filing affidavits of address change and denying their right to vote in the precincts in which they now resided. We will never know exactly how many times it happened and how many voters were affected, but in a state with a 1.2% margin of victory in 2016 every vote truly counted in awarding Florida's 29 electoral votes.

In addition to the infuriating acts of voter suppression that occurred, two other incidents that day should have told me the election was not going to end well for Hillary. The first one was a video that went viral on the news during the day that showed Trump supporters attempting to block other voters from going inside a polling place in Florida. When I watched it on my phone the location of the poll site flashed on my screen. It was a few miles away from my polling place. The whole area had the stench of Trump supporters who thought voter suppression was a good way to win an election. We would all learn with time that cheating, lying and stealing was the Trump way.

A second sickening incident took place at my precinct in the afternoon. Three older white men arriving for their tennis game at the club spotted me with my election protection sign hanging over my suit and advising some African-American voters outside the 100-foot mark. As they passed and got closer to the tennis court to the left of the poll entrance, they turned around and started chanting in a loud chorus, "lock her up, lock her up". Such disrespect for the sanctity of a polling place. Such contempt for the voter and me. No one knew at the time that obnoxious, uncivil behavior would become the theme for the next four years at the White House.

The polls closed at 7:00 PM and I was relieved that it ended. Jane and I helped dozens of voters with issues that they probably would not have successfully navigated on their own so that was very important. We alerted headquarters to that monumental suppression issue that got partially resolved so that was a victory. We outed an awful poll worker whose conduct only affected African-American and Latino voters. That outing is always a plus and hopefully raised a red flag about hiring him in the future (they do get paid apparently even when their actions suppress votes). I got through the indignities of the three rude, old and loud chanting white guys and the two white Trumpsters in the morning spewing their hate in hushed tones. I was ready to pick up my dinner, go back to the hotel and get redemption with a Hillary victory as the Trump campaign nightmare would fade into the dust bin of history. Oh well.

The allegedly "leaked" exit polling during the day was very encouraging for Hillary. There was not a whiff of a loss being reported. The discussion centered on how many of the swing states she would take and if she could get Arizona, Georgia and North Carolina in addition to the Rust Belt to make it an Electoral College landslide. The daytime pundits were quite certain about that in their analyses.

So I drove back to my hotel with a stop at the one pizzeria I had been to for the third day in a row. It was very close by to my hotel and the only place in the area that was not a fast food chain. It was a bit disturbing that the teenager who took my order three days in a row in an empty takeout place still didn't remember me. She didn't remember the same order each time I gave it either so I shouldn't be surprised. She also told me her family doesn't vote, so we hit the trifecta of the disengaged.

My car didn't have satellite radio so I was limited to the local radio stations on my dial on the ride home. Since Florida polls closed at 7:00 PM, it was quite early for results nationwide. I figured Virginia would be called immediately at 7:00 PM but it was listed as "too early to call". I thought this a little strange with Tim Kaine on the ticket and Hillary a lock to win the state. I chalked it up to the networks still being very cautious after 2000. Florida of course is usually a squeaker so that one I expected to be a much later call.

As I listened further North Carolina was also not called for Hillary immediately but I concluded since the latest North Carolina pre-election polling was a dead heat, it was just another close Hillary victory that would take some time. A little surprising, but when I would get back to my hotel room to watch MSNBC and CNN I'm sure it would be fine.

I called my wife in the interim and she said the TV pundits seemed a bit concerned that Trump was outperforming his polls in a lot of states. I told her and our sweet dog Bingo not to worry. The country is not going to elect a racist, misogynist, xenophobic con man and failed businessman. It would be closer than we would like but that's not going to happen.

When I got back to the hotel room I started to understand what my wife meant. There was a palpable concern in the voices of the commentators on both MSNBC and CNN. They seemed to know something that they weren't yet saying. The fact it took until about 10:30 PM for Hillary to be the projected winner in Virginia was really disturbing.[88] North Carolina fell and the pallor of the commentators kept getting more pale as every minute passed.

My wife was beside herself on the phone a few minutes after 11:00 PM as Florida came in for Trump.[89] I was sick. I dealt with that despicable poll worker all day long and he won in that end. Very disheartening.

With Wisconsin, Pennsylvania and Michigan fading, the die had been cast.[90] Within a number of hours into the early morning the alleged blue wall of states in the rust belt narrowly, but resoundingly were projected for Trump and a stunning and fateful day was in the books. By about 2:45 AM Hillary conceded since the Electoral College victory was sealed.[91] Virtually every pundit got the swing states wrong. Virtually every pollster got the Electoral College numbers wrong. The country, in my view, really got it wrong.

I was watching TV in my room turning from channel to channel to make sure it was real. CNN, MSNBC, FOX, CBS, ABC, NBC. Unanimous agreement that the unthinkable was a reality. I literally felt ill. I was stupified that the country could support someone who was an obviously unqualified fool and a bold purveyor of hate. It seemed so surreal. I stayed up for his speech which worsened my Trump-induced illness since it confirmed the reality of the election. I fortunately dozed off about 4:00 AM with the TV on hoping to wake up to a miracle.

A few hours later I rose and the TV was on replaying the nightmare of Election Day. I was appropriately depressed. The voters in the crucial swing states sorely disappointed me. The Florida voters crushed me. How could our country let this happen? Don't voters realize elections have consequences? However, none of us could have seen into the future that such catastrophic consequences beyond our worst fears were on the horizon.

I slowly packed my bags and headed to the chief election protection law firm in Fort Lauderdale to drop off some of my hard copy voter complaints from yesterday. It did feel like a morgue in the firm. I would say numb was my state of mind as I drove from that office to the airport. I kept replaying Election Day at the polls in my head since it was alarming to experience the level of voter suppression (intended or not) on the scale I observed in South Florida. That rerun followed by a close Trump victory in Florida and the three rust belt states (Wisconsin, Michigan and Pennsylvania) still left me in a bad dream sequence as I arrived at the airport. It was such an empty day after Election Day compared to 2008 and 2012. I was upset at the Bush victories in 2000 and 2004 but this felt like a new level of low. Those elections were very questionable and we ended up with the wrong leader in my opinion. This time, it seemed we had left the universe of contested politics and entered a *Twilight Zone* episode where the village idiot is put in charge. It would of course, turn out much worse than that. An evil and corrupt idiot with power is a dangerous combination as we now find out every day.

I flew home to a very disheartened Florence and our wonderful dog Bingo, but at least we were together to share the sadness of Hillary's defeat. I clearly remember the rest of that week unfolding with scenes on the news of thousands of protestors in the street chanting "Not my president" and " We don't accept the president-elect" in New York, Miami, Madison, Portland, Raleigh and other cities around the country.[92] I kept shaking my head over and over again as I yelled at the TV screen "Did you vote? Did you vote? You had your chance to stop this on Tuesday. Did you vote?"

My best guess is that many of the young people exercising their First Amendment rights in the streets may not have voted when it counted on Tuesday. One data analysis after the election showed that if just the 18-24 year old voters had voted in the percentages of those 65 and older, Hillary would have likely won Florida and Michigan making her the Electoral College winner by a 277-267 margin.[93] While I am not a data scientist and cannot vouch for the accuracy of that statistical study, I can tell you what I observed anecdotally coincides with that study. The numbers of young voters never seem to match those of older people at the polls.

But it's not just young people at all. I talk with lots of people of all ages from many different walks of life. In 2016, I heard so many of them before the election say things like, "I just don't like Hillary. I hate Trump but she's going to win anyway so why vote?"; "What's the difference who wins so I don't need to vote"; or "My vote doesn't affect my life so who cares if I don't vote?".

Every one of those statements I heard over and over again leading up to the election. Whether it was canvassing for Hillary in Florida, making phone calls for Hillary to swing states or listening to conversations in my office building elevator in Manhattan, I heard these sentiments over and over again. I could not help but think that many of those well-meaning protestors gave up their precious right to vote on Election Day for those same illogical reasons. They understood resistance the day after the Election Day debacle, but then it was far too late. Resistance in the streets after Election Day is no substitute for voting on Election Day – the ultimate act of resistance.

I now cancelled our Inauguration weekend reservations to see the installation of our first female president. We went from electing our first African-American President to electing a miscreant who would bring in an era of hate, corruption, ignorance, division and unparalleled incompetence. And we did it why? I will leave that answer to the political historians of the future but my simple answer is we got complacent, we assumed Hillary would win and some foolishly bought the propaganda that the village idiot would surround himself with qualified people and move the country forward.

Since I would not be writing my annual Inauguration celebration email to my friends, I decided after almost a week of mourning the election results, I would pen a different kind of email message that I entitled "Don't Whine, Volunteer":

"Dear Friends:

I spent last weekend and Election Day outside polling sites in Broward County, Florida on behalf of the Clinton campaign in my role as a volunteer lawyer poll observer. My job was to observe, resolve and report voting issues that could lead to disenfranchisement of voters (disproportionately, as always, African-American and Latino voters). I'll share more about my Florida experiences a bit later in this email.

We likely share the same feelings of shock and devastation at Tuesday's defeat of Hillary Clinton. I feel both shame and disappointment for the country I love so much. The majority of the Electoral College vote (popular vote totals aside), whether out of frustration or anger, chose hate, fear, racism, xenophobia, anti-Semitism, misogyny, anti-immigrant fervor and bullying over our core values of equality, justice, fairness, diversity and generosity. The seismic shock waves of this election will

likely be felt for years to come by our fellow Americans
and the world at large.

It is heartbreaking to imagine the nightmares that
now may be realized by some of our most vulnerable
neighbors. Will the ignorant bullies at school feel even
more emboldened to intimidate the little Muslim-
American girl whose perceived threat to them is her
different religion and culture? Will the little Mexican-
American boy whose parents are hard-working, undocu-
mented immigrants lose sleep every night worrying that
his parents will be taken away and deported? Will the
young African-American man continue to be the target
of discriminatory profiling and violence both directly
and systemically? Will the vulnerable single mother lose
her Obamacare and become a casualty of repeal without
a plan? Will the financially strapped blue-collar worker
become even more disheartened and disaffected if the
promise of immediate manufacturing and factory jobs
turn out to be a hollow campaign promise? Will the mil-
lennial entering the job market continue to drown under
the debt of college loans? Will the woman who now has
choices have the clock turned back on Roe v. Wade and
be denied the full services of Planned Parenthood? Will
respect for every woman be an ongoing casualty of the
vile campaign ran by the Republican President-elect?
Will our next generation's environment be eviscerated by
climate change deniers for the sake of fossil fuel energy
company profits?

The frightening answers to these important questions and others do not only affect the above groups of Americans, but they affect every one of us who love freedom for all, justice for all, and equality for all. In the words of the late civil rights hero Fannie Lou Hamer, "... nobody's free until everybody's free".

My Florida poll observation experiences offer some insight into our challenges ahead. On the bright side, my inside poll observer partner [Jane] and I were able to ensure that dozens of voters who were initially told by poll workers that they could not vote due to registration "technicalities" (a/k/a intentional or unintentional voter suppression) were eventually able to cast their votes after our interventions.

On the dark side, [Jane] and I observed numerous instances of systemic voter suppression created by laws established by Republican politicians and executed (intentionally or inadvertently) by allegedly "nonpartisan" poll workers. All of the suppression that we observed solely affected African-American and Latino voters. Proving intent is always a high legal bar, but it is beyond my imagination to think the disparate impact upon minority voters was a mere coincidence.

Voter suppression is not a particularly sexy issue for most members of the media. When Trump supporters allegedly blocked voters at a nearby poll on Tuesday, the media gave it coverage because there were available pictures and a reported police response. When systemic legal/technical issues happened at polls like mine, media attention was virtually non-existent because it is a far more nuanced story that cannot be described in a sound bite or captured in a photo or video. The latter type of voter suppression is a much more prevalent, pernicious and systemic problem that can easily result in hundreds of thousands of votes not being cast nationwide. The very votes that are not cast due to under the radar voter suppression can easily turn a swing state from red to blue.

To its credit, the Clinton voter protection headquarters was very responsive to our concerns at our polling place. There was a prioritized effort to involve the appropriate election officials. At times during the day things improved, but at other times it reverted back to the same suppression problems that we recognized earlier. Vigilance by all poll observers is a never-ending requirement to ensure fair and free elections.

When the polls closed, I read reports of similar problems of legal/technical suppression issues that were occurring in Miami-Dade County and Palm Beach County simultaneously with our experiences in Broward County.

We will never know if voter suppression efforts - intentional or inadvertent - changed the ultimate results in Florida, North Carolina and other swing states. We do know that one vote suppressed in our democracy is one vote too many. All eligible voters should be allowed to vote and all votes should be counted. That's called a free and fair election.

The next four years are not likely to unfold as we imagined when the pre-election pollsters and pundits assured us that a victory for Hillary was at hand. The next administration will test our confidence in our government institutions and democratic principles. We must be vigilant, focused and more active than ever in our participatory democracy moving forward.

I have a passion for protecting voting rights that led me to voter protection volunteer work at the polls and in the courts during the past twelve years. The Al Gore voting debacle in Florida in 2000 woke me up to this stain on our democracy. I hope my volunteer work makes our democracy a little better every election year.

Your passion for helping others may involve issues of child protection, domestic violence, elder care, homelessness, racism, education or an infinite variety of other societal problems. There are so many wonderful organizations that are begging for you to volunteer your services to help others. Just a few of those that come to mind are NationalPopularVote.com (reforming the Electoral College to honor the popular vote without the necessity of an act of Congress), NAACP, Planned Parenthood, ACLU, National Coalition for the Homeless, Brennan Center for Social Justice. Also, any local organization that provides services for the most vulnerable among us would love to have you as a volunteer to ensure that we as a society one day eliminate domestic abuse, poverty, discrimination of all kinds, injustice, homelessness, bullying, educational inequality, unequal pay for women and hatred in any form.

Remember, we're all in this together. Social change and social justice are only achieved when we all do our part. Our fellow residents of America need help. They need lots of help. Freedom comes with responsibility. We each need to do our part until equality, justice and fairness becomes a reality for everyone living in America.

Let's make everybody free. We're Americans. We get up when we're knocked down and come back twice as strong. Adversity creates character and the American character has no peer.

I implore you to adopt my new post-election motto: **DON'T WHINE, VOLUNTEER.**

Respectfully,
Richard C. Bell"

For my part, I of course continued my volunteer voting rights work, got involved as a regular donor to some dog rescue charities, school charities and medical charities and made it my mission to speak to every person I come into contact with daily about registering to vote and casting their ballots. If you are in an elevator, sitting next to me at an airport or standing in line next to me at a 7-11, you have probably heard me ask, "Are you registered to vote? Are you going to vote? Do you know your vote is so important that the entire 2000 election was decided by 537 votes out of more than 5.8 million votes cast?"[94]

I won't let it go and you shouldn't either. Every time an eligible voter doesn't register or doesn't vote it means someone else gets to decide the election. Bush or Gore? Bush or Kerry? Trump or Clinton? No one can convince me that the arc of history didn't change because of who was elected President due to how many people who did not bother to participate in the process. Only 56% of eligible voters voted in the 2016 Presidential election which ranked the U.S. a disgraceful 26th out of 32 highly developed democratic countries in the world in voter turnout.[95]

Think about that for a moment. Not even 60% of eligible voters made the decision to elect Trump over Hillary while the other 40% sat on their hands and watched it happen. In a democracy that is unforgivable apathy. I have said it ad nauseam because it can never be said enough times. Many have died for the right to vote. Many have struggled for the right to vote. Large swaths of our population, particularly African-Americans and women, were denied the right to vote for centuries. 44% of the voting population in the country thought it was too much of a bother to either mail in an absentee ballot or go to a polling place to have their say? I don't get it, but that portion of the public has sure felt the consequences of their apathy in the past 3 ½ years.

Before I move onto 2018, I will plead, beg and yell again at the top of my lungs, vote like your life depended on it because it does in so many ways that we have seen unfold in a few short years since 2016.

CHAPTER NINE

2017 AND 2018:

THE POWER OF VOTING – PASS IT ON

The damage being done since Trump's election has filled volumes of books, newspapers and digital media. It has become its own ratings bonanza for cable TV and talk radio. It has come so fast and furious that the critics never seem to catch up with it before the next dam bursts wide open with the sewage of his lies, hateful speech and policies.

From caging children to spewing racist rhetoric to defending neo-Nazis to bowing to the wishes of his revered Putin, the list is almost without end. A fantastic piece in *The Atlantic* magazine recounted the words of its prescient editorial in October 2016, about a month before the election:

"In an October 2016 editorial, *The Atlantic* wrote of Donald Trump: 'He is a demagogue, a xenophobe, a sexist, a know-nothing and a liar.' We argued that Trump 'expresses admiration for authoritarian rulers and evinces authoritarian tendencies himself.' Trump, we also noted, 'is easily goaded, a poor quality for someone seeking control of America's nuclear arsenal. He is an enemy of fact-based discourse; he is ignorant of, and indifferent to, the Constitution; he appears not to read.'

In retrospect, we may be guilty of understatement.

There was a hope, in bewildering days following the 2016 election, that the office would temper the man – that Trump, in short, would change.

He has not changed.

This week marks the midway point of Trump's term. Like many Americans, we sometimes find the velocity of chaos unmanageable. We find it hard to believe, for example, that we are engaged in a serious debate about whether the president of the United States is a Russian-intelligence asset."[96]

This excellent piece went on to reference 50 articles from *The Atlantic* on Trump's destructive presidency ranging from the lie on day one about the Inauguration Day crowd size to being an apologist for the murder of an American journalist by the Saudis and everything in between.[97] This mid-term assessment came shortly after the Democratic rout in the November, 2018 elections.

Suffice to say I, like many Americans, am infuriated daily by the man who will surely be judged by history at the bottom of the Presidential ladder. While commentators have often judged James Buchanan, Andrew Johnson, Franklin Pierce and Warren Harding on the bottom rung, Trump is the leading contender for worst ever in so many categories.[98]

Bemoaning his stupidity and damage to the country is a luxury I cannot afford nor can the rest of America (Admittedly, I still do it for a much longer period of time each day than I should.). By 2017, we all knew that Russian interference with the 2016 election certainly played a role in the useful idiot's victory (useful only to Putin). We also knew that there was almost nothing we could accomplish legislatively with a Republican House and Senate so that meant the 2018 midterm elections were going to be our next best chance to bring some accountability back to Washington before the cesspool of unprecedented corruption and incompetence flowed over into every aspect of our lives.

My focus, as it had been since shortly after the election, was to make everyone I could aware that elections count and their resistance in marches, social media and community organizing events were marvelous, but none of it counted if those marchers, drivers of social media and organizers did not mobilize and vote on Election Day. How many times do I need to remind you that the ultimate act of resistance is voting?

Getting out my message of volunteerism and resistance meant going beyond my own personal and professional circles. I needed to find an expanded audience. One day I came across this great charity on my Twitter feed that allowed schoolteachers to solicit funds for class projects that were not funded by the school budget (a sad but common occurrence in America). I contributed to a couple of them since the projects seemed very worthwhile and they were in inner city schools composed of children from low income families without the means to supplement the school's budget for special projects.

One particular project I read about in 2017 involved an art class that needed funding for supplies to complete a mural honoring the graduating class. It sounded very interesting and would certainly be a helpful way to engage students. I made a modest contribution to help the teacher reach her funding goal. After the goal was met, I received a lovely thank you response from the teacher.

In my response back to her, I mentioned to the teacher that if she were interested I would love to speak to the class about the field of voting rights and social justice during these perilous times. She was very receptive and we set up a meeting with her and a colleague who taught a law class at their public high school here in Manhattan.

When we met, I began to further understand how important the art project was to the students. Their art teacher explained to me that through the project they would learn the skills of brainstorming, researching, creating, negotiating and completing a large project as a team. Their beautiful tapestry would be a backdrop for the 2018 graduation and would be a source of pride to the students who would complete the journey from a creative idea to a tangible work of art.

Moreover, I learned that the majority of the students were African-American and Latino (many from first generation immigrant families) and came from homes with very difficult financial and social circumstances throughout New York City. They all came to this school for an enriching educational experience and some would be the first high school graduates in their families. College would hopefully become an attainable dream for those who did not have any close family members with college degrees.

In addition to the art class, the law class also invited me to speak the same day. It was a great opportunity to get out the message of voting as resistance to any part of the status quo that they opposed. It was not about their particular political views, it was about taking whatever political views they had and turning them into the change they wanted by voting. Voting is for Democrats, Republicans, Independents and any other affiliations or non-affiliations chosen by the voters. Resistance really means resistance to the powers that obstruct the changes you want and need. Period.

After meeting with these very dedicated and informed teachers, we set up the talk for early March 2018. As it turned out the timing was fortuitous. I met them a little more than three weeks after the deplorable shooting and slaughter on Valentine's Day 2018 at Marjory Stoneman Douglas High School in Parkland, Florida. 17 dead, 17 injured in another school shooting.[99] I was sure that this senseless catastrophe was an issue they, as high school students, could unfortunately relate to on a deep level.

I was very excited to speak to these students. I knew they were the sons and daughters of the very voters I had been protecting for the past 14 years and the children of the vast majority of the clients I represent in my law practice. Unfortunately, it was quite possible at some point in their lives due to their race they would face some obstacles in voting. I looked at this as an opportunity to both educate and empower the next generation about their rights and obligations as citizens.

When I got to the school that morning it was quite enlightening for me. I had not been in a high school for decades. When I went to high school in the 1970's there were no metal detectors, security guards and admittance procedures to get into the building. All of these things were now an accepted part of the school culture for good but tragic reasons. It felt a bit daunting to be entering the halls of education while passing through a security screening process worthy of a major airport. I understood the need for it, but felt a real sadness that every generation moving forward will experience this level of necessary protective procedures.

I was, of course, dressed in my lawyer-approved suit and tie. It was important to present professionally since my speech was about the law and social justice. They are very serious topics and my attire needed to reflect that theme of the talk.

I was escorted to the classroom which had a fascinating artsy beat to it. The students were on a break period but some were in the room mixing materials (Paints? I'm just a lawyer so I really have no idea.) and immersing themselves in the creative process. They and their teacher could not have been more welcoming and friendly during my early arrival. It gave me a chance for some one-on-one talk to learn about their class project and their present work. It was a fascinating introduction to high school circa 2018.

While so much had changed on the surface (like security and fashion style), the basics remained the same since my high school days. The usual teasing, giggling and playful interactions among the students was very reminiscent of my teen years. That was actually very refreshing.

The proverbial bell rang (that never changes I guess) and the art class of approximately 20 something students commenced. As I got up to the podium, I looked out at my audience and it reminded me of the jurors in all of my trials as a personal injury/medical malpractice/civil rights attorney. Some looked very curious. Some looked awake but distracted. Some looked like they wanted to be anywhere else but there. In other words, the usual sampling.

I began by telling them that I wanted to share my experiences as an attorney to educate them on the topics of voting rights protection and moving the needle of social justice forward as well as exploring the keys to professional, academic and personal success. The teachers and I decided that these students, in particular, needed to hear all of these messages. Since they came from tough circumstances and rough neighborhoods, they needed to know that they had all the tools necessary for personal and professional success, but had to hear the message straight and with honesty from someone in the legal and social justice arena. Many of them traveled on multiple buses and subways every day to get to school to receive the education they were entitled to. They needed support and encouragement that their daily sacrifices would pay off in the long run of life. My duty was to make them understand the possible was not a dream, but an achievable reality. They needed to work hard, study hard and remember there will be many obstacles thrown at them, but none that they could not overcome with focus and perseverance.

That all sounds good when I write it now, but I'm not the teenager living in a cramped apartment with parents working two low wage jobs and the streets around me filled with the evil forces of gangs, drugs and despair. For many of these bright kids that is the environment they return home to every day. My brief encounter with them would hopefully make a tiny difference since even a little bit is sometimes a lot. I know this personally from being lucky enough to have had inspiring teachers and professors throughout my years as a student in addition to very involved, loving and dedicated parents.

I started by telling them about Dr. King's reverence for voting rights as **"the foundation stone for political action"**.[100] I relayed my voting rights stories from Cleveland, New Jersey, Florida and Pennsylvania. I emphasized the importance of temperament and respectful verbal disagreement in my court interactions in New Jersey and my police incident in Philadelphia. I also hammered home the point that intense study and preparation allowed me to succeed in those voting rights cases in court and outside the polls. I must have repeated the words "study", "preparation" and "temperament" enough times to make their young heads dizzy.

I told them the value of staying calm and respectful even when I thought the judge was mean-spirited and wrong. I reminded them that the goal was to be heard, persuade and win. Raising my voice, losing my temper or being disrespectful to a judge was never going to achieve my goal of restoring a voter's right to cast her ballot. On the contrary, it could land me in jail where I was of no use to voters.

Similarly, I could have screamed and become irate at the lying poll worker in Philadelphia who called the police to arrest me. I explained to them that staying calm while the poll worker was out of control set the tone for the police listening to me. A calm and reasoned voice is always better in a tense situation. The goal was continuing to help voters to vote, not to get myself arrested and leave voters without an advocate and a source of vital Election Day information.

I told them what I told those Duke senior seminar students 5 years before. Moving the needle of social justice forward just a little bit is a very big deal. While the legendary names in social movements have a vital role, the real change happens when ordinary citizens do their part to move that needle of change forward, just a little bit. Each little bit on top of other little bits create a whole pile of social change. Small deeds by all of us combined move the needle from a little bit to a lot over time.

I did not simply *ask* them to get involved in causes dear to them. I told them it was their *duty* as productive members of society to do so. As young forces in their communities they were morally bound to make social change a priority when they see injustices and wrong-headed policies in society. I emphasized that whether it was volunteering to do voter protection, fighting to uphold the rights of immigrants (many of the students were sons and daughters of first generation immigrants), registering new voters (including themselves on their 18th birthday) or volunteering/marching for the causes of their choice it was incumbent upon them to participate in democracy, not remain a spectator. They needed to hear the profound words of Dr. King that are posted on my office cabinet, **"Injustice anywhere is a threat to justice everywhere."**[101]

I actually saw the faces become more animated as the speech went on. Not all. High schoolers are a tough crowd so I learned. Many, however, seemed genuinely interested in my message. I moved on to a discussion about their road to academic, personal and professional achievement. It was a three-part formula – constant study, lots of preparation and a calm, even temperament. I offered them some practical examples from my law practice.

As a trial attorney who presents cases to juries all over New York City, I emphasized that being intimately familiar with every aspect of the ever-changing law in my fields of personal injury/medical malpractice/civil rights were essential. How else could I know what questions to ask a client that will get me the relevant and important facts I need to know and how to fit the facts into existing law? That is true for construction law, auto accident law, sidewalk defect law, police brutality law and nursing home abuse law. Preparation is preparation no matter what the subject matter.

I surprised them with the fact that being a student did not stop with high school, college or law school. Studying for depositions, negotiations, motions, trials and appeals was a forever form of school homework. Being a dedicated student is a life-long pursuit. There is no shortcut to gaining knowledge, being educated on the latest developments and simply being the most prepared lawyer at the deposition, negotiation or trial.

Temperament is another critical tool in the quest for success, professionally and personally. Being calm and professional on the outside when you are bursting inside to slug your opposition is everything. I let them in on an open secret.

No adversary, judge or client will listen to me, respect me or follow my reasoned logic if I lose my temper. Very simply, civilized and educated people win arguments by respectfully presenting their arguments in a clear, logical and concise manner. We do not yell. We do not berate. We do not bully. Those kinds of people always lose in the long run in both the professional and personal worlds.

I pounded away that there is no such thing as studying too hard, being over-prepared, acting too professional or being too respectful when making an argument. I compared success and failure in the classroom to success and failure in the courtroom regarding all of those traits. Every one of those qualities works in the classroom, the courtroom and in the game of life. As I concluded my talk and opened up the room to questions, I hoped that I had reached at least one of them on some level because that was my job. Opening one young mind is one of the greatest gifts adults can give to youth.

The Q&A session did not start off well. There was an eerie silence that left me with the emptiness of a comedian whose audience never laughs. Tough start. I looked around the room. Moving onto eye contact with them individually got a mild reaction at best. I made some humorous (in my head), self-deprecating comments about their reaction to the speech. I threw out my best material to get at least one person to raise a hand with a question.

I looked over to one young woman and said, "Come on, you have to help me out here". She was my lifeline. Fortunately, it turned out she had ambitions of becoming a lawyer (Bing. Bing. Bing.) and didn't know whether in college there was a pre-law major or another path. Perfect first question. I congratulated her on wanting to enter my noble profession. I made it clear I was a history major and my fellow lawyers had majored in physics, history, biology, English and every other imaginable academic area. Her eyes widened like saucers. She had no idea that was possible. We had a detailed discussion about the point of college being a time to expand one's mind and breadth of experiences, not narrow it with a concentration in one discipline. I assured this curious student that her particular academic interests might change many times during her high school years and college days. And that was a good thing. A very good thing.

She was thoroughly engaged and intent on asking multiple follow-up questions. Her inquiries were crisp, pointed and important. I was sure to encourage and support her dreams and goals about entering the legal profession. She was bright and eager to learn. I answered all of her questions about college, studying methods and course selection in great depth. She was the symbol for a generation of learners, activists and leaders. From her questions, I realized that she had heard every word I said about social justice, voting rights and the qualities needed to achieve goals. I was on cloud 9. I really reached someone who started out shy (like the rest of the class at the Q&A) but sparkled with enthusiasm by the end.

Just like a fire, it only takes one spark. Now a number of hands went up and I was just thrilled with the responses. A young man asked if I was scared about being arrested in Philadelphia. I told him I was more scared of those poll workers continuing to deny voters their right to vote. He seemed surprised that a potential arrest (which I, of course, tried to avoid with calm) was secondary to protecting voting rights. I told him when you are on the side of right and passionate about an issue, you are willing to accept the consequences of righteous action. He really liked that stance and I saw a few other nods of approval.

The next question was also excellent. A student unknowingly set me up for a sermon. He wanted to know, if kids like him (black and brown kids from tough inner-city circumstances) could really challenge power as one person and one voter. I told him to look no further than the surviving Parkland students who were about his age. I told him "You hold all the power. Politicians are terrified of you. You and your peers can swing an election and put them out of a job. Your generation has the power to hire and fire politicians just like the Parkland kids in a matter of weeks pushed the Florida legislature to enact a three day waiting period on gun purchases by 18- to 21-year-olds.[102] Florida, a very pro-gun state, was never going to pass that law before the pressure came from those courageous, activist students who suffered the trauma of the Valentine's Day shooting in their school.

He was shocked to hear he and his fellow 14-18 year olds actually hold the power. This was a class composed of 95% students of color. I needed to be very direct and from the heart with them. "A bunch of old, white politicians in suits are not the power of the future. They're not even the power of today for much longer. You hold all the cards (I pointed to them individually). You are not just the future, you are the present. When you mobilize, when you march and vote in droves you resist their power and replace it with your power. In twenty or thirty years the demographics of this country are going to be you as the majority. Now is the time to own your power because the politicians that don't listen to you now will be in the graveyard of politics very shortly. Seize your power. Use your power. Volunteer. Protest. Run for office. Vote. Vote. Vote. Vote in local elections, statewide elections and national elections. Why do you think I need to do voter protection on behalf of African-American and Latino voters? Because certain politicians are terrified of you casting your votes in big numbers and replacing them with people who care about you and your fellow citizens and who believe in equality, justice and a truly free society. Don't ever think you don't matter in the scheme of things. You actually matter so much that there are forces out there specifically trying to suppress your right to vote. If you didn't matter in the political sphere, do you think they would spend all that time and effort trying to stop you from voting? Never forget you are the power but you have to use it. Social justice activism is fantastic to raise awareness and promote change. Voting is your ticket to making change real in the laws on the books. Never forget that".

The kids were kind of shocked I think that a white lawyer in a suit was telling them they are the center of power but just don't know it yet. I believe from the bottom of my heart that is true. I believed it then and I believe it even more now in light of the recent turning point for real change as a result of the cold-blooded murder (I understand a jury will decide that legally but we must use the strongest terms to describe this heinous act) suffered by Mr. George Floyd and its societal aftermath. I hope that the young man who asked that question was in the streets as a peaceful protestor in 2020 and at the ballot box as a dedicated voter year after year once he was eligible to vote.

The questions kept coming and I could not have been happier. These kids were terrific. It may have been an art class, but the real art was their creation of a figurative canvass of intellectual inquisitiveness, youthful enthusiasm and hope. What a great way to spend my time that day.

It wasn't over though. I had to answer the bell for the next class period with the law class of sophomores. The art feel disappeared quickly as I entered a clearly more serious and disciplined environment. The teacher had left the practice of law to teach young high school minds about the law so this was going to be a very different group.

The students in this larger class (closer to 30) were directed to shake my hand as they entered the room and introduce themselves to set a very business-like tone. I thought it was an excellent lesson in business world etiquette. It also broke the ice for me with individual students before my address.

I gave the same talk as in the art class, but this group had been advised to come prepared with questions so silence was not an option at the end of the lecture. They had prepared written questions in their notebooks for me. That led to an intense and fruitful discussion.

The first person to ask a question was a young African-American woman in a middle row. She said the class had been reading, *The New Jim Crow: Mass Incarceration in the Age of Colorblindness* by Michelle Alexander. I think she asked the following provocative question to test my authenticity as a white guy in a suit speaking to black and brown kids about civil rights and social justice, "We are reading 'The New Jim Crow' book and I believe slavery still exists, what do you think?" I walked up the aisle, stood a foot away from her, looked her straight in the eye and said, "Of course slavery still exists on some level but it's just in a different form. It comes with shackles and chains in the prison system, but it comes in insidious and invisible ways in the form of systemic racism in the worlds of education, justice, voting rights, economics and healthcare. Of course you are right and that is why we all have to fight the struggle for social justice every day by volunteering our efforts for important causes, marching in protest when we disagree with policies and laws and voting, voting and voting to change leadership who write our laws and enact policies in our names. Great progress has been made in 400 years, especially since the 1960's civil rights and voting rights legislation, but great challenges lie ahead to eliminate the present vestiges of slavery."

I could physically feel her sense of shock, relief and trust. I told her my most deeply held beliefs about societal norms, power and the ability to make change. She already knew where she stood, but I think she was very surprised that I stood with her. Just because I have not lived her life, felt her experiences and been on the victim's side of systemic racism doesn't mean I cannot understand the core of its evil, the poisonous roots of its nature and the rot it spreads on the fabric of a society that strives for equality and justice. We cannot solve these 400-year-old problems without everyone being on the righteous side of the issue of oppression. That means a role for members of every race, religion, ethnicity, gender, sexual identity and on and on. I wanted her to understand that we need to all hold hands and march together because we either all rise or all fall together. Fannie Lou Hamer rises in this book again, **"Nobody is free, until everybody is free"**.[103]

What this student did not know is that my late Dad told me a horrific story of prejudice that he faced in the late 1940's. He was the son of first-generation Jewish immigrants. After his service in World War II, he went to college and was a stellar student. Not just very good, but stellar. In his junior year in college he was named the top-ranking student in his class that year. He had a keen mind for business and graduated as a distinguished student in business administration. When he graduated, he was granted an interview with a large, prestigious company. The interview was going off the charts as he described it. At the end came an ugly question that was allowed in that era, "What's your religion?" When he said he was Jewish, the interviewer's jaw dropped.

As my father recounted it, the man was shocked because our family name, Bell, "didn't sound Jewish" to the interviewer. The tone of the conversation completely changed. My Dad was told he was by far the best qualified candidate. His academic credentials were impeccable. His business acumen during the interview was superb. His people skills were terrific. He was perfect for the sales department job. Well, almost perfect. The man told him if it was up to him the job was my Dad's on the spot. Unfortunately, the interviewer said the company "doesn't hire Jews". That's just the way it was and he was sorry for that but he just couldn't hire him because company policy is company policy.

Instead of becoming discouraged, my Dad went onto another company that did not discriminate based on religion and the rest is history. He was a self-made, highly successful businessman who owned his own business for many decades. He also helped put many people into business in his field of import-export that others shunned due to their ethnic and religious backgrounds as immigrants from India, Pakistan and other regions. He never forgot the discrimination he felt and made sure to do the right thing when it was his turn to be in power. I am deeply proud of the heritage I came from. My Dad, Mom and my Grandparents (Don't get all rules of style on me. These are all capitalized under my own rules out of my deep respect for them.) all lived through eras when antisemitism was in your face and widespread. They all taught me right is right. Discrimination is an infectious disease if you don't cure it. No one should be judged by what they look like, what religion they believe in or where they grew up. Everyone is entitled to the same opportunities, the same dreams and the same freedoms. I was brought up to believe that and it is deep-seated in my heart, mind and soul. If that young woman ever reads this book, maybe she will have a better understanding of why her battle is my battle and why I get her without having been her. So I have digressed. Not really.

The rest of the class Q&A was fantastic. The kids wanted to know if I was tempted to punch the poll worker, "I was but besides not being productive, punching someone 6 inches shorter and 30 lbs lighter wasn't a fair fight anyway. Just kidding. Violence is not an option. Ever." They understood. They even laughed.

Another student wanted to know if poor people could afford a lawyer if they had a potential lawsuit for personal injury/medical malpractice/civil rights. What a softball question for me. I explained that I worked on a contingency fee which meant I only get paid if I win. They had apparently never heard of this. It led to a great discussion about my field of law.

I explained that one of the things I loved about being a plaintiff's lawyer in my field was that I get to represent people from all walks of life. Unlike corporate lawyers, tax lawyers and other business lawyers, I have the honor of representing regular people regardless of their economic status. I told them that the vast majority of my clients over the years have been people of color from neighborhoods in Brooklyn, Queens, the Bronx and Manhattan that most fancy law firms have never heard of or visited. I let them know I was honored to be a voice for people hurt in housing authority buildings, public hospitals and dangerous construction sites but who did not have money to hire a seasoned trial attorney. Since I don't charge clients any upfront fees and they only pay fees out of the proceeds of a winning result, the poorest person gets to choose the best lawyer. The only criterion is the merits of the case, not the size of one's bank account. To me, that is a level playing field as I explain in my previous book, *WHY insurance companies HATE when you hire a lawyer.* Plug noted.

They were genuinely shocked to hear that news. Also, when I told them I visited many a client and accident site in areas of the city not usually frequented by white guys in suits they were pleasantly surprised. I needed them to know pre-judging a white guy in a suit as necessarily an establishment authority figure out of touch with their communities

175

was not a good idea either. We all need to see each other as human beings first and foremost. We need to celebrate our different backgrounds of race, religion, ethnicity, sexual orientation, etc. and bask in our cultural diversity. We also need to recognize our vast community as all members of one race, the human race. We will never achieve our goal of a just and equal society if we do not have brutally honest discussions and an unvarnished exchange of ideas and reforms about race and its pervasive place in our history and society. When we drop our preconceived perceptions to deal with each other person to person we open up a whole world of possibilities many of us have never imagined. I think the kids understood that we were actually more alike than different in our basic values despite some of our different life experiences.

The questions never stopped even after the bell rang for the next period. A few kids came up to me with more questions about the law, voting and social justice. They were real. They were passionate. They gave me great hope for the future.

By the time it was over, I was high from the excitement of interacting with these special kids. It was an exhilarating day that restored my faith that even in the age of Trump and his hatred, lying and incompetence there was a generation out there that was ready to do something about it. I walked away more determined than ever to fight for the rights of everyone wrongly denied them by forces I consider to be the essence of evil.

A few weeks after our discussion, a large envelope arrived at my office with a return address of the high school where I gave the talk. When I opened it and read the contents, my eyes welled up with the knowledge I may have moved the needle of social justice, if just a little bit.

I will share some of the notes written by these wonderful students not to demonstrate that I did something good. That is not the point. The real purpose of letting you in on the following is that kids from every walk of life are starving for information, knowledge, support, recognition, respect and engagement. Their curiosity is endless. Anyone who thinks it is any different in a public school in America's largest city with the vast majority of students of color from low income backgrounds needs some schooling themselves. These kids were stellar in their level of involvement in the classroom discussion and obviously absorbed some lessons that will help them on their road to intellectual, professional and civic superstardom. Like all of us as youths, they just need people who care enough to guide them through the challenges of society like their very dedicated teachers, parents and community leaders. Their notes make me so proud to know them and so reassured that their generation will make things happen that my generation only dreamt about.

I present you a beautiful sampling of a Manhattan public high school's classes of 2018 and 2020[104]:

"Mr. Bell, Thank you for teaching me temperament. I have already applied temperament to my life and I feel in control when I'm calm and the other person isn't.";

"Thank you, Mr. Bell, for coming to our class and sharing your knowledge and experience that proved to be highly inspirational especially to help people.";

"Thank you for the knowledge you gave us on voting rights.";

"Thank you for spending your time speaking to us and giving advice on controlling our temper.";

"Thank you, Mr. Bell, for being so considerate and willing to come to teach us about the law.";

"Thank you for taking your time to talk to our classroom about the law and the certain techniques to be successful.";

"Thank you for coming and volunteering and giving us a lesson on voting rights.";

"Thank you for informing us about what you do. I've learned a lot about voting rights and thanks for the wonderful pens [art equipment] you donated to us. Keep on informing many more. Thank you!";

"Thank you so much for your inspirational words and coming in on your spare time to speak to us! I felt empowered to continue making change in the world.";

"Thank you for taking time out of your schedule to inspire all of us!";

"Thank you for your time and what you do.";

"Thank you for the inspiration on my artwork.";

"Thank you for taking the time off from your job and coming to enlighten us about the strength to vote.";

"Thank you for supporting us and taking time out of your day to talk to us. I honestly look up to you.";

"Thank you for lending your time to the students and being anti-electoral college!";

"Thank you for inspiring me even more to be a lawyer.";

"Thank you for standing up for what you know is right and donating to our graduation project.";

"Thank you for talking with us and fighting for the rights of our people.";

If those comments by the sons and daughters of mostly working poor families who are African-Americans, Latinos, immigrants from the Middle East and Central America, do not make you understand what is great about America I feel sorry for your lack of humanity.

These kids are not starting off in the game of life with privilege, high-income parents, private schools and traditions of family legacies at the top universities. They are starting with very little on a material level. They are, however, so rich in curiosity, awareness and hope for a better society. Anyone who ignores them or has such narrow racist thinking as to squelch their dreams and opportunities does so at his own peril. They are not just the boundless future of America, they are our hope in the present. They all turned 18 between 2018-2020. They are voters. They are ready to lead if politicians will not. They are the epitome of what is right about America.

Politicians who oppose equality and injustice, they're coming for your job. Now.

They probably taught me more than I taught them that day in the classroom. I listened to their concerns, their ideas and their opinions. They are smart. They are not going to let another generation hold them back because of race, religion or national origin. They are a force to be reckoned with for the next 70 years and America needs to wake up to the passion of their voices.

They really got it during our brief time together. They got the part about temperament in making their points. Temperament is not about being quiet during a protest march (my wife and I certainly weren't quiet a few weeks later when we participated in the March for Our Lives demonstration for gun control in Manhattan). It's about being respectful in a courtroom, a boardroom or a voter suppression encounter to persuade the decision maker that your opinion is the most persuasive, logical and correct. They got it. They will make this country great with their resistance to racism, inequality and environmental insanity. How? Protesting, organizing and mobilizing to exercise the ultimate act of resistance of their generation - voting.

CHAPTER TEN

Florida. I Can't Get Enough of You?

Now it was time to get back to my own role in the arena
of voting rights and social justice. As the mid-term elections were approaching, I was thrilled at the prospect of a
Democratic comeback in the House of Representatives. The
Senate still looked shaky.

After two years of the disaster for the ages known as the
Trump era, I was cautiously optimistic about the mid-terms.
With the Republicans holding control of the presidency,
House and Senate, there was no oversight of any kind over
the racist and xenophobe in-chief. Only a win in the House
would restore at least a partial semblance of accountability
as to what level of corruption, incompetence and mayhem
was really going on in Washington behind the curtain (so
much was going on in plain sight too). Having read Michael
Wolf's *Fire and Fury* in early 2018, Rick Wilson's *Everything*

Trump Touches Dies in summer 2018 and having consumed thousands of articles, interviews and podcasts about Trump's assault on our democracy, I was raring to go back to my voter protection duties in November 2018.

I had never travelled out-of-state for a mid-term election, but 2018 was different. If the Democrats could not take back the House, Trump and his spineless sycophants in the Republican Party would continue to defy the rule of law, sully the foundation of our basic democratic principle of fair play and desecrate what was left of our country's former policies on economic/healthcare inequality, racial discrimination and equitable immigration reform. We haven't even discussed the damage Trump did in two years to international relations, climate change policy and the courts. Suffice to say the destruction done in a very short time was breathtaking. While he had another two years on his term (No hope a Republican Senate would ever convict him if the House voted for impeachment), we needed Nancy Pelosi back in charge of the House as a partial counterbalance.

I looked around at the big races in each state and decided, for better or worse, I could do the most good in the bastion of poor elections, Florida. There was a very tight Governor's race predicted between Democrat Andrew Gillum (a big surprise winner of the Democratic primary) and Republican Ron DeSantis, the worst kind of Trump yes man in the House (he even had a commercial made where he told his infant son to build a wall using toy blocks).[105] Also, incumbent

Senator Bill Nelson was in a very tight race against former Governor Rick Scott (remember him from an earlier chapter when his discriminatory, disparate impact ex-felon order prevented so many African-Americans from voting in 2016?). I had to do my part to stop this continuing madness in the Sunshine State (not so sunny for Democrats, people of color and immigrants).

The best thing about Florida for me is that my voting rights partner Jane lives there and would be teaming back up with me on Election Day to try to get Florida voters to cast their ballots without obstruction from poll workers. The worst thing was that I was back in Florida where voting did not go so well in 2016 from my point of view.

This time we were assigned to a very large polling venue at a health club of all places. I guess it's a Florida thing. At least there was a juice bar inside and the poll workers this time were actually friendly. An unusually large turnout was expected since it was a hot year for the mid-terms due to a lot of anti-Trump sentiment in the country coupled with the two closely contested races for governor and senator in Florida. We were ready for action.

It was a blistering hot day on Election Day in Broward County in 2018. This was especially true for a guy in a suit and tie on the sunny side of the building. Despite a thousand comments on my attire from Floridians, "You must not be from around here", I was very comfortable with my choice of clothing. It projected a message of seriousness that

Florida could certainly use in its elections. There you go Florida. I said it.

I am pleased to report that this polling place in 2018 was not a repeat of my 2016 experience in Florida. That's not to say there were no issues. The morning started off with the same change of address issue as in 2016 but with a different twist. The poll worker was not questioning whether the registered voter who changed addresses within the county could vote at the polls, he was just misinforming them that they needed proof of address change as opposed to having them sign an affidavit of change of address within the county. This issue was limited to one poll worker, but it resulted in long delays for a few voters in the morning. Since the law was clear and the poll worker was absolutely wrong, Jane spoke to the poll worker about his misinformation. It did not seem to make a difference and he literally took two hours with one voter on the issue of an address change. Most voters would not be so patient to stick around two hours to vote (thankfully there are a lot of retirees in South Florida with flexible schedules). Certainly, as crowds grew during the day such a delay, if continued, would cause massive lines to form.

Jane got the message to me and I informed headquarters as to the problem. Jane astutely pointed out that once a poll worker gives out such misinformation to voters it could create a massive voter suppression problem. If the clerk is allowed to delay voters from voting it means long lines form and potential voters get out of line due to frustration and go home without voting. That's the kind of voter suppression that depresses the vote but rarely gets quantified. It is every bit as dangerous as denying someone the right to vote inside the polling place. Remember, long lines mean long waits means less people hanging around to actually vote especially in the hot Florida sun.

It took a few calls and some persistence but headquarters got the office of the Supervisor of Elections to lean on the poll worker and stop the damaging practice. I cannot say that there was any pattern of intentional racist discrimination in this potential voter suppression. I can say with a high degree of certainty that stupid isn't good either. Poor training and supervision of poll workers who work one day a year is fraught with danger. We spend millions of dollars setting up and administering elections and the training and supervision part of the process seems to be lacking. Adequate federal funding for professional training of poll workers I guess would be a fantasy in Mitch McConnell's Senate. The man who joins Trump as America's greatest threat to democracy literally used the words "this whole voter-suppression nonsense".[106] Enough said about "Moscow Mitch".[107] We don't want the stain of his name on these pages.

The rest of the day was fairly uneventful as far as voter suppression goes. There was a steady stream of voters from 7:00 AM to 7:00 PM with only a smattering of voter issues that all got resolved inside by Jane without the need for my further contact with headquarters. I was able to dispense some helpful advice to a number of voters who had ID questions, address change questions and some other miscellaneous problems. All were resolved in favor of the voter casting a ballot.

As usual, in my area 100 feet from the polling entrance I was stationed near people giving out pamphlets for their candidates. This was perfectly legal. Everyone was well behaved and civil. One guy looked familiar, but I couldn't place him. I then looked at the pamphlet he was passing out and realized he was the Republican candidate for the House seat in my polling place district. There was a lull in the afternoon and I approached him for a friendly talk. I said "You seem like a nice guy. You really believe that dismantling Obamacare, tax cuts for the rich and cutting health and safety regulations are good for South Florida and America?" He was really caught off guard by my question. He stumbled through some rote answers, but I wouldn't let him off the hook that easily. I asked how he could support a misogynistic, racist, xenophobic man like Trump. He back-pedaled again and mumbled some standard answer about not being partisan and being open to all points of view. He seemed entirely disingenuous and insincere. I guess I wasn't the only one that felt that way. The Democratic candidate trounced him at the end of the day. We had our friendly, civil exchange and I walked away very unimpressed.

There was also a nice young couple handing out campaign leaflets on the line. They were really interesting. Maybe it was the woman's Bronx roots (her family grew up there), but the three of us really clicked. She was very knowledgeable about Florida state politics and local issues. She had real insight into issues like the ex-felon voting rights order of Governor Scott and reasons why Florida could never seem to run elections right. I'll just say she was not impressed with the people in charge of the election apparatus throughout her years of political activism in Florida.

They were both Latino and expressed a disappointment with the lack of cooperation from diverse Latino groups to put together a unified coalition in South Florida. Her views on the dangers of splinter groups stopping the greater good from succeeding was enlightening. They knew a lot about the political climate and predicted that despite the latest polls, it would be extremely difficult for an African-American to win a statewide election in Florida and be elected Governor. They were also concerned that Rick Scott was going to win too. As an outsider, I may have had a skewed view of the possibility of Florida doing the right thing this time. They told me not to get my hopes up because the Florida electorate was a tough nut to crack for progressive Democrats due to its transient nature, Southern roots and a Republican legislature that set the rules of the game. Fascinating, but hopefully wrong. I still text with them to this day and they sure knew their home state.

So a semi-eventful morning turned into a smooth afternoon and evening. Jane and I assisted many voters with little resistance from the poll workers after the early incident. We felt good about our work, but Jane too warned me to not get too optimistic about the Florida electorate. What is in that Florida drinking water?

I wearily went back to my hotel room to once again watch the results. It had to be better this time, right? Let's start with the national results. Phenomenal. Democrats win a historic gain of 41 seats in the House with a cumulative national margin of over 8.8 million votes.[108] While election night results were incomplete, the victory was assured and the final results were a clear repudiation of Trump. Hallelujah.

Florida, oh dear Florida, not so in step with the nation. Florida flipped the Democratic senate seat by about 0.13% to Republican Governor Rick Scott who was a clear enemy of voting rights (Mr. I alone can stop African-American ex-felons from getting their right to vote restored – remember "disparate impact"?).[109] The governor's race was so close after the first count (less than 0.5%) it triggered an automatic machine recount that resulted in a DeSantis Republican victory by 0.40% - less than 34,000 out of more than 8 million votes cast.[110] By the way, DeSantis has been an unmitigated disaster during Covid19.[111] Will they never learn in Florida?

The country won. Florida lost. It was time for me to go home. Such a peculiar state. Always teasing with the close margins, but never delivering since my time there in 2016 (not to mention 2000).

I had one main mission in Florida in 2016 and 2018. I was there to make sure as many Floridians as possible had their right to vote protected by me. That part was accomplished. I also wanted to be a member of the winning team in the Florida elections. Not accomplished. The first goal was paramount so I walk away knowing I gave it my all. The actual electorate in Florida? You can still redeem yourself in my eyes and the eyes of much of the nation in 2020. Come on. Don't disappoint again. We're willing to forgive you. Barely. But still willing.

CHAPTER ELEVEN

FOR 100 MILLION AMERICANS, NO RESISTANCE MEANS STAYING HOME ON ELECTION DAY

You have now read a lot about voter suppression, resistance and civic involvement. That only tells a part of the story of voting rights in 2000 and beyond. The dirty little not so secret fact about voting in America circa 2016 is that "nearly 100 million eligible Americans did not cast a vote for president, representing 43% of the eligible voting-age population."[112]

That staggering figure has led to the Knight Foundation, funded by a famous newspaper publishing family and dedicated to the belief "an informed citizenry is essential for representative democracy to function effectively", creating *The 100 Million Project*.[113] This important study is meant to dive into a bloc of our nation that could change every election result moving forward if it participated in large numbers like the other 57% of our citizens.[114] That number of non-voters, 100 million, is unfathomable for someone who grew up in awe of the sacred right to vote.

While the non-voters are a complex group, the study indicates that these tens of millions of non-voters feel their votes don't matter, don't engage much in civic involvement, have less faith in the system and consume news less.[115] All of these conform with what many thought, but now we have some firm polling numbers that fall in line with the anecdotal evidence. So what do we do about it?

Firstly, even the worst and most evil forces behind voter suppression might find it extremely difficult to suppress another 50 million or 75 million voters if they showed up on Election Day. That's just math.

While there is no magic pill to get the non-voters to vote, maybe the unspeakable tragedy involving Mr. George Floyd and the federal government's (and some states as well – hey Florida, I'm talking about you) response to Covid19 may mobilize eligible voters who have either never registered or rarely participated in elections in the past. The millions who took to the streets to protest in support of the tenets of Black Lives Matter has been encouraging. The diversity of the marchers has given me hope that more of us understand the adage I keep getting back to since it capsules the whole point of this book, **"Nobody's free until everybody is free".**[116] I encourage you again to read more about Fannie Lou Hamer, one of the all-time legends in the voting rights and civil rights movement.

What a hero. And don't forget another voting rights legend of the civil rights and voting rights era, Congressman John Lewis whose recent death leaves a large hole in our hearts but is forever a reminder of what courage looks like and sounds like, **"When you see something that is not right, not just, not fair, you have a moral obligation to say something. To do something."**[117]

If the resistance of those who believe in Black Lives Matter, equal justice, economic equality, health care equality, environmental equality and voting rights equality is really committed to turn our nation's pervasive problems around we need look no further than the ultimate act of resistance – voting.

Many politicians care more about their elections and re-elections than the good of society and their constituents. Do you think Mississippi lawmakers removed the image of the Confederacy from its state flag after 126 years because politicians all of a sudden got a conscience?[118] Or do you think the outrage and persistence of protestors since the brutal killing of Mr. George Floyd moved public opinion so much that even white Mississippi politicians got the message that it is better to be on the right side of history with elections coming up?

Even in a liberal state like New York, do you think politicians all of a sudden got a conscience in June 2020 to do a ten bill package of long-talked about police reforms like outlawing chokeholds and opening up police disciplinary records to public scrutiny or was it the political pressure mounting from protests and marches every day and night in New York City in the wake of Mr. George Floyd's killing led by the Black Lives Matter movement?[119] Elections, as politicians well know, are coming soon in November 2020 and no one wants to be on the wrong side of public outrage. At least no one who wants to be elected or re-elected in vast swaths of America.

You really think that the timing and speed of these political moves are coincidental? Does public sentiment expressed in marches, protests, petitions, social media presence and wall-to-wall news coverage affect politicians who want to be elected or re-elected? Ask New York Democratic Congressman Eliot Engel whose district in the Bronx and Westchester was a lock for him for decades (he served 31 years).[120] He lost his seat in a primary landslide to a progressive African-American middle school principal and first-time candidate. "Engel's biggest sin: He almost never went home. Even during the COVID-19 crisis, when his district in the Bronx and Westchester County, New York was hardest hit, Engel stayed locked down in his home in suburban Maryland. The final straw may have come earlier this month when he showed up at a news conference about police brutality and was heard, on a hot mic, asking the MC, Bronx Borough President Ruben Diaz, if he could speak. When Diaz told him there was a long list of speakers, Engel said, 'If I didn't have a primary, I wouldn't care.'"[121]

All of the above informs me that the power of change by voting is at a frenzy if the public understands that their desperation and will for change really lies in their own hands – in registering, filling in and mailing a mail-in ballot or pulling a lever at a poll on Election Day. It's really that simple. The ultimate act of resistance is really only a vote away. Each vote on top of each other vote makes for a real change. Ask Al Gore how many votes it can take to win the presidency (537 by the way if you skipped that chapter).

Now we have a chance to mobilize the voting public and the usual non-voting public because of the dual disasters of the Mr. George Floyd on-camera murder (I know. A jury still has the final say to get it right.) and the raging pandemic that worsened for months under the lack of leadership of our do-nothing president. The public seems ready to rise to the occasion and turn to the ultimate act of resistance – voting. I sure hope so. And where are voter suppression efforts in the scheme of things for the 2020 election? Time to drop the flowery idealism and get real about where we are at the moment (I live for idealism, but I am steeped in reality especially based on my experiences in the world of voting rights and jury trials.)

How's that proposed voter registration boom going? According to Nate Silver's highly respected organization, FiveThirtyEight, since we entered the pandemic "new registrations have fallen off the cliff."[122] What? How can that be? While new voter registrations in January and February were up compared to 2016, that is now no longer true.[123] One explanation is that "in person registration at places like departments of motor vehicles made up a large plurality, or even a majority of new registrants in four places for which we have data on how new voters are registering. But after the pandemic caused most states to shutter many government offices, those registrations dwindled. . . the closing of schools and public events like festivals has hindered in-person voter registration drives run by third-party organizations . . . Voto Latino, an organization that works to register and engage Latino Americans to vote, has been operating digitally almost since its inception and was well prepared to continue its work during a pandemic. It uses digital campaigns to help voters register, which can even work in states like Texas, which does not have online voter registration – Voto Latino created an app that makes it easy to fill out the required form which is them emailed to the voter to print off and mail in."[124] While Voto Latino has had a surge in voter registration even during the pandemic due to its excellent digital infrastructure, the same is certainly not true across the board.[125] The survey by Five Thirty Eight concludes that the kinds of new voters not registering during the pandemic are "probably disproportion-ately young" and those total number of potential voters are not registering in line with 2016 numbers in two key swing states, Florida and Georgia.[126] If that continues, I don't need data scientist credentials to know that could be a major blow to fall voter participation in those two critical states.

While the magic pills to solve those issues are in our grasp, they are not likely to happen before November 2020. As discussed earlier, automatic voter registration states compose about one-third of the states voting and is unlikely to change any time soon.[127] By requiring registrants to "opt out" instead of "opt in", every interaction with the motor vehicle department or other state agency is the chance to automatically be registered and updated on the state's voter rolls.[128] It also means electronic transfer of voter registration information which prevents the paper registration form issues that at times end up becoming contested issues at polling places on Election Day.[129]

So easy, yet so resisted by more than two-thirds of the states to date. If it could ever become a sexy issue for the media and politicians who favor free and fair elections, we could go a long way toward putting voter suppression to rest. Unfortunately, this is a long-term goal that requires lots of state legislatures to actually want everyone to vote. If you've been paying attention to voting in America at all, you know massive voter participation is not every politician's goal. I'm talking to you Rick Scott and, of course, you Moscow Mitch. A special shout out to Governor Brian Kemp of Georgia who holds a special place in the voting rights hall of shame.[130]

Short of a legislative miracle in dozens of states, such reform is not a realistic goal for 2020. Of course, even when there are lots of registered voters on the books, people like then Secretary of State and now Governor Kemp like to do voter purges which in Georgia resulted in 1.5 million voters being purged from voting rolls from 2012-2016.[131] Purging and "cross-checking" (to determine if voters are registered in another state) is an effective voter suppression tactic since it removes one's name from the eligible voting list on Election Day many times due to failure to have an exact name match due to clerical error, misspelling or other erroneous reasons.[132] Do you think the purging of 16 million voters between 2014 and 2016 resulted in errors that disproportionately purged African-American voters and voters of color? Since the Voting Rights Act pre-clearance was eviscerated by the Supreme Court in 2013, writer Michael Harriot of *TheRoot.com* cites to the Brennan Center report on purges which "estimates *two million fewer* voters would have been purged if those states had to abide by the provisions of the Voting Rights Act of 1965."[133]

While noble and effective solutions are proffered by the venerable Brennan Center For Justice (Automatic Voter Registration, litigation to overturn violations of the National Voting Registration by unlawful purges and state legislation to at least inform voters they are being purged with adequate notice to correct errors) do you know how long those simple and effective reforms will take to be enacted?[134] Not in time for November 2020 for sure. When voters go to the polls in droves to elect officials who support voter suppression reform then the states and federal government will enact those laws that the Brennan Center rightly promotes. Voting – the ultimate act of resistance to politicians who perpetuate voter suppression.

In the meantime, I beg every person who is a citizen and 18 or older to do things like yesterday when it comes to their own voting rights. Go to the excellent non-partisan, non-profit website, **VOTE.ORG**. In a few clicks you can register to vote online if your state permits it or get the information you need to register if there is no online registration. If you think you are already registered, you can confirm that you are marked registered in your county's system and make sure you have not been purged. If you remember nothing else from this book, remember **VOTE.ORG**. It is an indispensible tool for every voter and potential voter.

If you think voter suppression on steroids isn't coming to a community near you, check out the news of the past few months. Do you recall the Wisconsin primary in April during the pandemic? The Democratic governor had issued a stay-at-home order, tens of thousands of voters had not timely received their mail-in ballots and on the eve of the primary Election Day the conservative Wisconsin Supreme Court ruled to block a court order extending the time to obtain absentee ballots.[135] Since hundreds of poll workers failed to show up on Election Day during a pandemic, National Guard troops were called in to staff them.[136] In a stunning and patriotic ultimate act of resistance, voters showed up in long lines to defy the obvious voter suppression tactics. As described by one brave voter "'We decided to risk our lives to come vote,' said Bradish, 40. 'I feel like I'm voting for my neighbors, all the people who don't have the luxury to wait this long.'"[137] This brave soul was not exaggerating since the Wisconsin Department of Health Services reported that "A total of 71 people got COVID-19 after voting in person or working at the polls during Wisconsin's April 7 election. . ."[138] While adequate tracing was not confirmed, it is a viable working hypothesis and no voter deserves to ever be at a potential health risk by exercising her right to vote.[139] It will come as no surprise that lack of poll workers in a pandemic resulted in Milwaukee's polling places on Election Day shrinking from 180 to 5 in a county where 70% of the state's African-Americans reside.[140] Ironically, a liberal democrat won an upset victory for Wisconsin Supreme Court justice on that Election Day.[141] Justice sometimes does prevail.

So at least we learned from the Wisconsin primary debacle in April by the time the Georgia primary came around in June, right? If you don't know the obvious answer, read this account of the Georgia primary in June:

> "It was impossible to watch Tuesday's election fiasco in Georgia – the equipment failures, the dramatic reduction in the number of polling precincts, the voting centers that failed to open on time, the insufficient number of paper ballots, the nearly seven-hour lines in many minority communities contrasted with the breeze in whiter, wealthier suburbs – without thinking, ruefully, of US

supreme court chief justice John Roberts' 2013 decision in Shelby County v Holder that ripped the heart from the Voting Rights Act.

Those interminable lines wrapped across Atlanta and many other minority counties? The waits almost as long as a workday, making a mockery of any notion of a free and fair election? Well, more than 200 precincts across Georgia, disproportionately in minority counties, have been ordered closed since Roberts and the US supreme court cast aside protections that had prevented states and localities with a history of racial prejudice in voting laws from remaking their electoral rules without federal oversight.

But it wasn't just in-person voting that malfunctioned on Tuesday. It was also impossible to watch Georgia's expanded vote-by-mail system meltdown – forcing tens of thousands of voters who requested, but never received, absentee ballots to either join these long lines at the remaining, understaffed precincts, during an ongoing pandemic, or forfeit their civic voice entirely – without envisioning a train wreck this fall. Not just in Georgia, but in Wisconsin, Michigan, Pennsylvania and many other crucial states where any repeat of the chaos we have already seen this spring could precipitate a constitutional crisis unlike any other in our history."[142]

I am not so shocked to learn that since the Voting Rights Act decision by the Roberts Court in 2013, ". . . more than

200 precincts across Georgia, disproportionately in minority counties, have been ordered closed. . ."[143] If you got this far in the book, you could have written that sentence yourself.

So now we have the usual voter suppression compounded by people's legitimate fears of going out to polling places with lots of crowds during the worst pandemic in over 100 years. What would a nation that cares about free and fair elections do? Offer every registered citizen a mail-in ballot and make the deadline for mailing it in be a postmark on Election Day. Simple and efficient, right? Ask the voters of Alabama whose mail-in ballot procedures during the pandemic are for the moment (the Supreme Court has granted a temporary stay allowing the state rules to stay in effect for now) requiring the undue burden of notarized mail-in ballots and a smart phone/printer to make copies of one's ID to mail in with the ballot.[144] You think that might tend to disenfranchise low-income and elderly voters who don't necessarily have access to such technology or the means to pay a notary?[145]

This is not a complicated problem to solve if we had elected officials who were interested in having every eligible voter registered, every ballot cast and every vote counted. A few years ago the *New York Times* editorial board reviewed the simplicity of solving the problem.[146] The aforementioned automatic voter registration idea nationwide is a no-brainer and it alone, if enacted by all states, has been estimated to add 22 million voters to the rolls yearly.[147] The editorial also restated many long argued reforms only now in force in a minority of states such as same day registration, online registration and pre-registration of high school students at 16 or 17.[148] An extension of early voting laws and making such early voting a mandatory option in all states would also expand voter participation significantly.[149]

If it's so obvious and easy to implement why do people like me still need to do voter protection election after election? Because there are political forces at work that do not want everyone registered and everyone voting for fear that it would cause their side to lose elections. As the transparent idiot-in-chief recently said about the proposals to increase funding for massive mail-in voting during the pandemic (and thereafter), "The things they had in there were crazy. They had things – levels of voting that, if you ever agreed to it, you'd never have a Republican elected in this country again."[150] Meaning, if democracy works and full voter participation is achieved that's somehow a bad thing? You got it.

The myths and lies spread by opponents of easy access voting and expansive participation is intended to create fear of totally imaginary voter fraud – the nonexistent boogeyman. Study after study and court opinion after court opinion have definitively debunked the myth of voter fraud and found such actual facts, based on data, that there are only 31 in-person credible instances of voter impersonation out of 1 billion votes cast; 4 documented cases of voter fraud in the entire 2016 election; "the likely percent of non-citizen voters in recent U.S. elections is 0".[151] The lies about voter fraud have been put to rest as a matter of data science and we are left with the following conclusion by a report from the revered Brennan Center for Justice:

> "The verdict is in from every corner that voter fraud is sufficiently rare that it simply could not and does not happen at the rate even approaching that which would be required to "rig" an election. Electoral integrity is key to our democracy, and politicians who genuinely care about protecting our elections should focus not on phantom fraud concerns, but on those abuses that actually threaten election security.
>
> As historians and election experts have catalogued, there is a long history in this country of racially suppressive voting measures — including poll taxes and all-white primaries — put in place under the guise of stopping voter fraud that wasn't actually occurring in the first place. The surest way toward voting that is truly free, fair, and accessible is to know the facts in the face of such rhetoric."[152]

Even Trump's own ridiculous voter fraud commission disbanded without producing any evidence of alleged massive voter fraud in 2016, leading to voting rights experts at the ACLU and the Brennan Center for Justice to conclude respectively it "was a show from the start" and it "started as a tragedy and ended as a farce".[153]

You must be both infuriated and exasperated already as to why we cannot get up to speed and let everyone have their voting rights in a quick, efficient, equal and fair manner, right? We should obviously follow all of the above recommendations that voting rights advocates have been promoting for years, correct? And certainly in the era of Covid19 mail-in voting should be accessible to all voters, shouldn't it?

The added attraction of vote-by-mail contained in a study of the 5 states that require universal vote-by-mail as the only way to vote - (Oregon, Washington, Colorado, Hawaii and Utah) – is that it favors neither party over the other.[154] California for the November, 2020 election will be sending mail-in ballots to all voters without them requesting it so there will be no necessity of coming to the polls on Election Day during a pandemic unless one so chooses to do so anyway.[155]

At present, a voter does not need to proffer an excuse to vote by mail in 29 states and D.C. in general elections, but 16 states do require an "excuse" to vote-by-mail (New Hampshire allows the Covid19 pandemic as a valid excuse now).[156] As the title of a recent article on fivethirtyeight.com predicts "Few States Are Prepared to Switch to Voting by Mail. That Could Make For a Messy Election."[157] Welcome to the 2020 American elections.

Let us not delude ourselves, however, that vote-by-mail is not also subject to a different kind of voter suppression. Mail-in ballot rejections can be based on failure to have exact signature matches (the arbiters are clerks, not handwriting experts), failure to sign in every place instead of one general place and mail delays in reaching the elections boards on time due to overwhelmed postal workers.[158] California's March 3, 2020 primary resulted in 102,000 mail-in ballots being rejected and Wisconsin had a relatively high number of 20,000 rejected mail-in ballots for its April 7, 2020 primary.[159] A lawsuit in New York by the League of Women Voters questioned the state's process of rejecting absentee ballots without giving voters the opportunity to fix harmless administrative errors.[160] With an expected large mail-in vote in November 2020 due to the pandemic, these numbers of rejected absentee ballots are alarming and time is running out to remedy the state election laws to streamline the vote-by-mail ballot process. The problems with voting in America are endless because our state legislatures and federal government never seem to get around to the most obvious solution – whether it's voting in-person or by mail make it simple, easy and efficient so everyone can vote freely and fairly.

More troubling is the propaganda and lies coming out of the White House about the vote by mail trend that needs to be implemented immediately as time is running out for the November elections.[161] Trump's allegation that vote by mail is a partisan tactic favoring Democrats is a flat out lie debunked by a May 6, 2020 study at Stanford University entitled "Universal Vote-by-Mail Has No Impact on Partisan Turnout or Vote Share".[162]

Trump has put into the minds of low information voters nonsensical lies about Michigan sending 7.7 million ballots illegally; Nevada mailing illegal ballots; and "You can't do the mail-in ballots because you're going to have tremendous fraud."[163] His words are worthy of a minister of propaganda when set against the facts.[164] One of the nation's foremost experts on elections, Richard L. Hasen, Professor of Law and Political Science, concluded that "absentee ballot fraud is very rare – there were 491 prosecutions related to absentee ballots in all elections nationwide between 2000 and 2012, out of literally billions cast. . . .Trump is throwing fuel on the fire and undermining the November election. It is up to the rest of us to keep dousing his flames with the truth."[165] Propaganda aside, there likely will be barriers put up by many states to deter widespread vote by mail during the pandemic in November 2020.

Just an additional note on a potential vote-by-mail issues for November. Our impeached (but unfortunately not convicted due to sycophant weaklings in the Senate) president has another cheating scheme up his sleeve. His newly appointed and, of course, unqualified Postmaster General is allegedly working on the following:

"The Postal Service plays an important role in ensuring that voters can cast their ballots by mail. In states that do not offer prepaid postage, the Postal Service still delivers ballots that do not require postage to submit. The Postal

Service works with state election officials to design the
ballots' envelopes to ensure a smoother process, and it
handles ballots differently from regular mail so every vote
is counted. But what happens if that cooperation slows or
breaks down? We are already seeing warning signs. Public
reports indicate that DeJoy [Postmaster General] is planning to eliminate overtime, which could cause delivery
delays and hinder voting by mail."[166]

That's right. Another thing to be concerned about for the
November election. Remember, it's much harder to complete
such a scheme if the public votes in droves and early. Early. In
droves. It takes away much of this form of voter suppression.
It's up to you.

You have now learned lots about how we can maximize
and streamline voting if we enact simple and clear laws like
any committed democracy should do. We have not done it to
date leaving voter suppression to be in full bloom on Election
Day 2020.

In fairness to the House of Representatives, it passed the
Voting Rights Advancement Act in December, 2019 restoring the pre-clearance protection from the 1965 Voting Rights
Act that the U.S. Supreme Court eviscerated in 2013 as well
as a section requiring public notice of registration changes
and allowing federal election observers to be sent nationwide.
Moscow Mitch, despite it being introduced in the Senate, has
not even allowed a hearing on the bill in the Senate to date

(That could change by the time this book is published so if it does that means even Moscow Mitch felt the pressure.). No surprise there.[167] The most extensive and widespread voter protection bill, H.R.1, passed the House in early 2019 and includes almost every voting reform we need at the moment:

"* Automatic voter registration
* Online voter registration
* Same day voter registration
* Make Election Day a federal holiday
* Voting rights restoration to people with prior felony convictions
* Expand early voting and simplify absentee voting
* Prohibit voter purges that kick eligible voters off the registration rolls
* Enhance election security with increase support for a paper-based voting system and more oversight over election vendors
* End partisan gerrymandering by established independent redistricting commissions
* Prohibit providing false information about the elections process that discourage voting and other deceptive practices"[168]

Bravo to the House. Where have you been for over a year while the bill sits on your desk Moscow Mitch?

What can you, the individual voter, do to make sure your vote counts? Be alert. Check your registration early to make sure you are in the polling "book" (**VOTE.ORG**). If you have not already registered or re-registered after moving, do it immediately to avoid problems on Election Day (**VOTE. ORG**). If you are required to go to the polls by state law or by necessity always look for voter protection advocates like me outside your polling place wearing a button or a sign (and hopefully a loud voice reminding you about your voting rights and resolving your problems at the poll). If you vote by mail, check and recheck the arcane instructions on your absentee ballot and follow the instructions to a T. I mean recheck three times to avoid having your ballot rejected.

After you read all of these pages advocating for voting rights and promoting your power as a voter, I must regretfully inform you that a frightening theory has been raised as to the worst-case scenario in this year's Presidential election. I warn you that the theory is extreme and unprecedented, but the times we live in leave us with an open mind about the possibility of bizarre.

We have covered the usual voter suppression tactics of purging voter rolls of largely African-American voters and other voters of color; suppressing vote-by-mail ballots with restrictive requirements on procedures (Alabama's notary and ID copy laws) deadlines (Election Day receipt as opposed to Election Day postmark); Election Day polling place challenges targeting African-American and other voters of color; long lines in urban areas created by reduced polling places; registration "errors" by poll workers or election boards that have "disparate impact" on African-American voters and people of color.[169] All of those are still in play. The next one requires you to put on your seatbelt.

I do not normally subscribe to conspiracy theories (though we are not in normal times), but consider what if an even more outlandish scenario ensues and Trump loses the election and literally invokes unprecedented emergency powers to stay in office.[170] What? Preposterous you say. Really? Sit down and have plenty of fluids as you read about this nightmare unfolding as envisioned in a recent opinion piece on *newsweek.com*:

> "1. Biden wins the popular vote, and carries the key swing states of Arizona, Wisconsin, Michigan and Pennsylvania by decent but not overwhelming margins.

> 2. Trump immediately declares that the voting was rigged, that there was mail-in ballot fraud and that the Chinese were behind a plan to provide fraudulent mail-in ballots and other "election hacking" throughout the four key swing states that gave Biden his victory.

> 3. Having railed against the Chinese throughout the campaign, calling Biden "soft on China," Trump delivers his narrative claiming the Chinese have interfered in the U.S. election.

4. Trump indicates this is a major national security issue, and he invokes emergency powers, directing the Justice Department to investigate the alleged activity in the swing states. The legal justification for the presidential powers he invokes has already been developed and issued by Barr.

5. The investigation is intended to tick down the clock toward December 14, the deadline when each state's Electoral College electors must be appointed. This is the very issue that the Supreme Court harped on in *Bush v. Gore* in ruling that the election process had to be brought to a close, thus forbidding the further counting of Florida ballots.

6. All four swing states have Republican control of both their upper and lower houses of their state legislatures. Those state legislatures refuse to allow any Electoral College slate to be certified until the "national security" investigation is complete.

7. The Democrats will have begun a legal action to certify the results in those four states, and the appointment of the Biden slate of electors, arguing that Trump has manufactured a national security emergency in order to create the ensuing chaos.

8. The issue goes up to the Supreme Court, which unlike the 2000 election does not decide the election in favor of the Republicans. However, it indicates again that the December 14 Electoral College deadline must be met; that the president's national security powers legally authorize him to investigate potential foreign country intrusion into the national election; and if no Electoral College slate can be certified by any state by December 14, the Electoral College must meet anyway and cast its votes.

9. The Electoral College meets, and without the electors from those four states being represented, neither Biden nor Trump has sufficient votes to get an Electoral College majority.

10. The election is thrown into the House of Representatives, pursuant to the Constitution. Under the relevant constitutional process, the vote in the House is by state delegation, where each delegation casts one vote, which is determined by the majority of the representatives in that state.

11. Currently, there are 26 states that have a majority Republican House delegation. 23 states have a majority Democratic delegation. There is one state, Pennsylvania, that has an evenly split delegation. Even if the Democrats were to pick up seats in Pennsylvania and hold all their

2018 House gains, the Republicans would have a 26 to 24 delegation majority.

12. This vote would enable Trump to retain the presidency.

We cannot let ourselves believe that this is a far-fetched scenario. We have just seen Trump threaten to invoke emergency powers under the Insurrection Act of 1807 to call up the U.S. military against domestic protesters. The remarkable apology by Joint Chiefs Chairman General Mark Milley, stating that it was wrong to create a perception that the military would get directly involved in a domestic political protest and intervene against American civilians, underscores the corrupt use of executive powers Trump is willing to employ. As Fareed Zakaria recently said in summing up the lessons of former national security adviser John Bolton's new book: "Donald Trump will pay any price, make any deal, bend any rule, to assure his own survival and success."[171]

Wild and crazy conspiracy theory by two alarmists? Maybe. Plausible and logical theory by two realists? Maybe. We will never know until it's too late, right? So what do we do to make that opinion piece a work of fiction?

The answer is obvious. Do the ultimate act of resistance to ensure this never happens in 2020 or at any point in our history – VOTE. Don't just register to vote in good numbers. Register to vote in historically record-breaking numbers.

Don't just vote by mail (if afforded the chance in your state) or in person (if required or necessary in your state) in good numbers. Vote in unprecedented numbers that would be the envy of countries with mandatory voting. The most effective way to avoid that horror movie of an "emergency powers" nullification of an election (i.e., full on dictatorship) is to vote in such overwhelming numbers that there are no close vote totals in any state. Landslide victories have no basis for challenge. That is true in votes for President, Senate and the House as well as state and local elections. Record voter turnout and record winning margins should turn the above opinion piece into nothing more than an interesting class-room discussion in political science 101.

If you haven't already noticed in the past 3 ½ years, elections always have consequences. They have consequences for your daily life and the lives of your family, friends and neighbors. Want to attack systemic racism as a structural long-term change? Vote to elect politicians who prioritize the reforms you want. Want to attack the rising scale of econom-ic inequality in America? Vote to elect politicians who will enact structural, long-term reform. Concerned about police brutality disproportionately affecting African-Americans and people of color? Vote to elect politicians who support your vision of structural, long-term reform. Want America to lead (or at least to join) the world on the fight to combat the effects of global climate change? Vote for politicians who share your vision and will enact laws accordingly. Tired of worrying about bankruptcy from a medical emergency because there is no real universal health care or Medicare for All? Vote for politicians who support making this law. Frustrated with student loans burying you in debt? Vote for politicians who will pass laws that lessen your burden. Tired of watching the super wealthy and monstrous corporations getting the big tax breaks and you getting the scraps? Vote for politicians that will make your views the law. And if you disagree with every one of the above propositions, all that clearly represent my personal point of view, then vote in droves for politicians who support the opposite views. As is my rule in my voter protection work, I support every voter being allowed to vote and I will fight for every voter regardless of her political position since voting is a right for all not for some.

Resistance is different things to different people. Resistance may be resistance to the status quo. Resistance may be resistance to changing the status quo. All that matters is that you voice your power with the ultimate act of resistance – voting.

Also, the power of voting is vital when politicians run for re-election. If the candidate made promises that she didn't keep, you need to hold her to her word and vote her out if she didn't do what you thought she would. That's the power of the individual voter.

My passion is voting rights if you haven't guessed by now. I love voting. I love it even more when everyone's right to vote is protected and exercised. I love when everyone participates in our democracy with vigor and enthusiasm. We are in a moment that cries out for competent leadership to get us through the worst pandemic in one hundred years as it has left a staggering death toll and a shredded economy due to lack of leadership, planning and implementation of basic public health standards. We are in a moment of real potential for a fundamental shift in racial justice in all aspects of society. We are in a moment when a global pandemic has accentuated our broken economic and health care system. Our poor level of voter participation in the past cannot be repeated in 2020 because the epic decision of our future as a democracy should not be made without every citizen's input. If the first 6 months of 2020 have not taught us that we need each other more than ever to exist, survive and thrive as one peoples, we have sadly missed the point of the dual crises of racial inequality and Covid19. Now is our time to move more quickly and honestly to a more perfect union. There is no more American way to do it than voting. It is your right. It is your duty. It is your present. It is your future. Don't let others decide for you. Don't sit out the most important election of our time. Vote for the kind of America you dream about because you have the power to make that dream come true for generations to come. Marches and protests have done a phenomenal job of raising awareness and getting some initial laws passed. You want the real reform that comes from laws and policies that help push forward fundamental and structural social justice change? Vote. Voting is the ultimate act of resistance. Do it!

I leave you with the words of two heroic resisters who paved the way for so many millions to gain the right to vote:

"Someone struggles for your right to vote. Use it." Susan B. Anthony.[172]

"Whether you have a Ph.D. or no D., we're in this bag together. . ." Fannie Lou Hamer.[173]

CHAPTER TWELVE

ABOUT THE AUTHOR

Richard C. Bell has been practicing law in New York City since 1982. In 1986, he opened his own practice focused on personal injury/ medical malpractice/civil rights and he has maintained that practice based in Manhattan since that time (*www.877calllaw.com*). He represents clients in cases resulting from negligence, including auto accidents, construction accidents, medical malpractice, police brutality, nursing home negligence, fall downs, product liability and more. Mr. Bell handles all aspects of his cases, from the initial investigation through settlement, trial verdict and appeal. He is motivated by a true sense of concern for his clients and a desire to get them the compensation they deserve by fighting to make sure those responsible are brought to justice. Though he is a tough trial attorney, he treats his clients with respect and compassion because he understands the personal tumult they are experiencing.

He is the author of *WHY insurance companies HATE when you hire a lawyer.* It is a consummate primer on what to expect when you bring a personal injury/medical malpractice lawsuit in New York City.

Mr. Bell has been interviewed by major media networks and publications about his cases and as a legal analyst which include the following: CBSNews.com, New York Post, CNBC.com, The Laura Coates Show, ABC7 TV (San Francisco), Jet Magazine, BusinessInsider.com, WCCO Minneapolis, San Diego's Morning News – KOGO, KTRS – St. Louis, KMOX – St. Louis, The Jim Bohannon Show, Middays with Perri Small – WVON, KGO San Francisco – Consumer Talk, Healthline.com, This Morning with Gordon Deal, WTAM – Cleveland, WLW – Cincinnati and Inside the Issues with Dr. Wilmer Leon – Urban View.

His pro bono love is voting rights. He has been on the ground at the polls and in the courtroom defending people's right to vote since 2004 in Ohio, New Jersey, Pennsylvania and Florida. He will not be happy until election protection attorneys like him are no longer needed on Election Day.

Mr. Bell graduated Magna Cum Laude from Duke University. He then received his Juris Doctor from Rutgers University School of Law. While at Rutgers, he served as the Features Editor for the Rutgers Journal of Computers,

Technology, and the Law and was a member of the Rutgers Moot Court Board. Upon graduation, he was admitted to the New York Bar as well as the New Jersey Bar. He has also been admitted to the U.S. District Court – Southern District of New York, Eastern District of New York, Northern District of New York and District of New Jersey. He is a member of the New York State Trial Lawyers Association, New York Academy of Trial Lawyers and the New York State Bar Association.

Mr. Bell has also participated in speaking engagements at a number of prestigious conferences in Barcelona, Cancun, San Francisco and Washington, D.C. He has also been honored by Super Lawyers, The Million Dollar Advocates Forum, National Academy of Personal Injury Attorneys and Top Attorneys of North America.

COMMUNITY INVOLVEMENT

In addition to his trial law practice and voting rights work, he has also done extensive pro bono work, including representing the estate of a 9/11 victim before the Federal September 11th Victim Compensation Fund through the Trial Lawyers Care organization and has been recognized by the New York Firefighter's Burn Center Foundation for pro bono work. He also will come up to you on the street or in an elevator and ask if you are registered to vote and will you be voting. That is not a joke.

NOTES

ACKNOWLEDGMENT

1   Chris Carson, "Celebrating Dr. Martin Luther King", *League of Women Voters*, January 15, 2017, https://www.lwv.org/blog/celebrating-dr-martin-luther-king-jrs-legacy.

2   "Fannie Lou Hamer Quotes and Sayings", www.inspiringquotes.us.

3   "State Felon Voting Laws", December 18, 2019, www.procon.org.

CHAPTER ONE

4   Linda Mason, Kathleen Frankovic, Kathleen Hall Jamieson, "CBS News Coverage of Election Night 2000, Investigation, Analysis, Recommendations", (*The Annenberg School for Communication, University of Pennsylvania*, January 2001).

5   Ibid.

6   Ibid.

7   Ibid.

8   "Election 2000 Timeline", *Pittsburgh Post Gazette*, www.post-gazette.com, December 17, 2000.

9   David Firestone, "Contesting the Vote: The Overview; Supreme Court, Split 5-4, Halts Florida Count in Blow to Gore", *The New York Times*, December 10, 2000, https://www.nytimes.com/2000/12/10/us/contesting-vote-overview-supreme-court-split-5-4-halts-florida-count-blow-gore.html.

10   Bush v. Gore, 531 U.S.98, 144 (2000); Michael Herz, "The Supreme Court in Real Time: Haste, Waste, and *Bush v. Gore*", 35 *AKRON LAW REVIEW* 185 (2002)

11   Ibid.

12   Jeff Desjardins, "Mapped: The World's Oldest Democracies", *World Economic Forum*, August 8, 2019. https://www.weforum.org/agenda/2019/08/countries-are-the-worlds-oldest-democracies

13   "Bush wins second term as Kerry concedes", *CNN*, November 3, 2004, https://www.cnn.com/2004/ALLPOLITICS/11/03/prez.main/index.html.

14   Ibid.

15   "Preserving Democracy: What Went Wrong in Ohio", Status Report of the House Judiciary Democratic Staff, January 5, 2005.

16   Ibid, 4.

17   Ibid.

18   Ibid, 4-6.

19   Ohio Secretary of State, www.ohiosos.gov.

20   Grace Panetta and Olivia Reaney, "Today is National Voter Registration Day. The evolution of American voting rights in 242 years shows how far we've come – and how far we still have to go", *Business Insider*, September 24, 2019, https://www.businessinsider.com/when-women-got-the-right-to-vote-american-voting-rights-timeline-2018-10.

21   William Chafe, Raymond Gavins and Robert Korstad, *Remembering Jim Crow* (New York: The New Press, 2001).

22   Voting Rights Act of 1965, https://www.ourdocuments.gov/doc.php?flash=true&doc=100.

23   Help America Vote Act of 2002 (HAVA), *U.S. Election Assistance Commission*, https://www.eac.gov/about_the_eac/help_america_vote_act.aspx.

24   Ibid.

CHAPTER TWO

25   Theodore R. Johnson, Max Feldman, "The New Voter Suppression", *Brennan Center for Justice*, January 16, 2020, https://www.brennancenter.org/our-work/research-reports/new-voter-suppression.

CHAPTER THREE

26   "Disparate Impact Discrimination", December 4, 2018, https://employment.find-law.com/employment-discrimination/disparate-impact-discrimination.html.

27   Ibid.

28   www.census.gov.

29   Afran v. County of Somerset, 244 N.J. Super. 229 (App. Div. 1990).

30   "What is Same-Day Voter Registration", March 23, 2020, https://www.findlaw.com/voting/my-voting-guide/same-day-voter-registration.html.

31   Max Feldman, "10 Voter Fraud Lies Debunked", *Brennan Center for Justice*, May 27, 2020, https://www.brennancenter.org/our-work/research-reports/10-voter-fraud-lies-debunked and "Debunking the Voter Fraud Myth", *Brennan Center for Justice*, January 31, 2017, https://www.brennancenter.org/our-work/research-reports/debunking-voter-fraud-myth.

CHAPTER FOUR

32   Afran v. County of Somerset, 244 N.J. Super. 229 at 231-232 (App. Div. 1990).

33   "Disparate Impact Discrimination", December 4, 2018, https://employment.find-law.com/employment-discrimination/disparate-impact-discrimination.html.

34   "Voter Turnout", *Fair Vote*, https://www.fairvote.org/voter_turnout#voter_turnout_101.

CHAPTER FIVE

35   "New Jersey to Press Forward with Motor Vehicle Implementation", *Press Release by State of New Jersey, Department of the Public Advocate*, March 24, 2018.

36   Ibid.

37   Ibid.

38   Ibid.

39   Ibid.

40   42 U.S. Code Section 1973gg (1993)

41   "N.J. voting officials scramble to process record number of registrations", October 21, 2008, https://www.nj.com/news/2008/10/nj_voting_officials_scramble_t.html.

42   "This is your victory", Transcript of Barack Obama's Victory Speech, *CNN*, November 5, 2008, https://edition.cnn.com/2008/POLITICS/11/04/obama. transcript/.

43   "10 Fannie Lou Hamer Quotes to Celebrate Her 100th Birthday", *Because of Them We Can*, October 6, 2017, https://www.becauseofthemwecan.com/blogs/culture/10-fannie-lou-hamer-quotes-to-celebrate-her-100th-birthday.

44   Ibid.

CHAPTER SIX

45   Vann R. Newkirk, II, "How Voter ID Laws Discriminate", *The Atlantic*, February 18, 2017, https://www.theatlantic.com/politics/archive/2017/02/how-voter-id-laws-discriminate-study/517218/; Jasmine C. Lee, "How States Moved Toward Stricter Voter ID Laws", *The New York Times*, November 3, 2016, https://www.nytimes.com/interactive/2016/11/03/us/elections/how-states-moved-toward-stricter-voter-id-laws.html; Max Feldman, "10 Voter Fraud Lies Debunked", *Brennan Center for Justice*, May 27, 2020, https://www.brennancenter.org/our-work/research-reports/10-voter-fraud-lies-debunked and "Debunking the Voter Fraud Myth", *Brennan Center for Justice*, January 31, 2017, https://www.brennancenter.org/our-work/research-reports/debunking-voter-fraud-myth.

46   Jasmine C. Lee, "How States Moved Toward Stricter Voter ID Laws", *The New York Times*, November 3, 2016, https://www.nytimes.com/interactive/2016/11/03/us/elections/how-states-moved-toward-stricter-voter-id-laws.html.

47   Ibid.

48   "Voter ID: Applewhite v. Commonwealth", *The Public Interest Law Center*, May 2012 – May 2014, https://www.pubintlaw.org/cases-and-projects/applewhite-v-commonwealth/.

49   Ibid.

50   Ibid.

51   Ibid.

52   Ibid.

53   Ibid.

54   Ibid.

55   Applewhite v. Commonwealth of Pennsylvania, No. 330 M.D., 2012, 2014 WL 184988 (Pa. Commw. Ct. Jan. 17, 2014).

56   "Automatic Voter Registration, a Summary", *Brennan Center for Justice*, July 10, 2019, https://www.brennancenter.org/our-work/research-reports/automatic-voter-registration-summary.

57   Ibid.

58   Ibid.

59   "Audio and Transcript: Obama's Victory Speech", *National Public Radio*, November 7, 2012, https://www.npr.org/2012/11/06/164540079/transcript-president-obamas-victory-speech.

CHAPTER SEVEN

60   Chris Carson, "Celebrating Dr. Martin Luther King", *League of Women Voters*, January 15, 2017, https://www.lwv.org/blog/celebrating-dr-martin-luther-king-jrs-legacy.

61   "Martin Luther King Jr. Memorial Quotations", National Park Service, https://www.nps.gov/mlkm/learn/quotations.htm.

62   Shelby County Alabama v. Holder, Attorney General, Et. Al., 557 U.S.193 (2013).

63   Shelby County Alabama v. Holder, Attorney General, Et. Al., 557 U.S.193 (2013); Adam Liptak, "Supreme Court Invalidates Key Part of Voting Rights Act", *New York Times*, June 25, 2013, https://www.nytimes.com/2013/06/26/us/supreme-court-ruling.html.

64   Adam Liptak, "Supreme Court Invalidates Key Part of Voting Rights Act", *New York Times*, June 25, 2013, https://www.nytimes.com/2013/06/26/us/supreme-court-ruling.html.

65   Ibid.

66   Michael Cooper, "After Ruling, States Rush to Enact Voting Laws", *The New York Times*, July 5, 2013, https://www.nytimes.com/2013/07/06/us/politics/after-Supreme-Court-ruling-states-rush-to-enact-voting-laws.html.

67   Vann R. Newkirk, II, "How Voter ID Laws Discriminate", *The Atlantic*, February 18, 2017, https://www.theatlantic.com/politics/archive/2017/02/how-voter-id-laws-discriminate-study/517218/.

68   Zoltan Hajnal, Nazita Lajevardi and Lindsay Nielson, "Voter Identification Laws and Suppression of Minority Votes", *The Journal of Politics*, University of California San Diego, 79, no. 2, pp. 369-379 (April 2017).

69   Jasmine C. Lee, "How States Moved Toward Stricter Voter ID Laws", *The New York Times*, November 3, 2016, https://www.nytimes.com/interactive/2016/11/03/us/elections/how-states-moved-toward-stricter-voter-id-laws.html.

70   Ibid.

71   "Provisional Ballots: An Imperfect Solution (Issue Brief)", *The Pew Center on the States*, July 2009, https://www.pewtrusts.org/~/media/legacy/uploadedfiles/pcs_assets/2009/elecprovballotbrief0709pdf.pdf.

72   Ibid.

73   Max Feldman, "Dirty Tricks: 8 Falsehoods That Could Undermine the 2020 Election", *Brennan Center for Justice*, May 14, 2020, https://www.brennancenter.org/our-work/research-reports/dirty-tricks-9-falsehoods-could-undermine-2020-election.

74   Ibid.

75   Ibid.

CHAPTER EIGHT

76   Adam Gabbatt, "Golden escalator ride: the surreal day Trump kicked off his bid for president", *The Guardian*, June 14, 2019, https://www.theguardian.com/us-news/2019/jun/13/donald-trump-presidential-campaign-speech-eyewitness-memories.

77   "Jane" is not her real name. She will be referred to as Jane throughout the book. She still has to live in Florida so her identity will remain anonymous.

78   Monivette Cordeiro, "Rick Scott restored the voting rights of twice as many white former felons as black felons", *Orlando Weekly*, October 31, 2018, https://www.orlandoweekly.com/Blogs/archives/2018/10/31/rick-scott-restored-the-voting-rights-of-twice-as-many-white-former-felons-as-black-felons.

79   Editorial Board, "Florida restored voting rights to former felons. Now the GOP wants to thwart reform", *The Washington Post*, January 13, 2019, https://www.washingtonpost.com/opinions/florida-restored-voting-rights-to-former-felons-now-the-gop-wants-to-thwart-reform/2019/01/13/84e2dcdc-1520-11e9-803c-4ef28312c8b9_story.html.

80   Abby Goodnough, "In a Break from the Past, Florida Will Let Felons Vote", *The New York Times*, April 6, 2007, https://www.nytimes.com/2007/04/06/us/06florida.html.

81   "Roadblocks to Restoring Rights", *Sarasota Herald-Tribune*, March 14, 2011, https://www.heraldtribune.com/news/20110314/roadblocks-to-restoring-rights/1.

82   Monivette Cordeiro, "Rick Scott restored the voting rights of twice as many white former felons as black felons", *Orlando Weekly*, October 31, 2018, https://www.orlandoweekly.com/Blogs/archives/2018/10/31/rick-scott-restored-the-voting-rights-of-twice-as-many-white-former-felons-as-black-felons.

83   Ibid.

84   Ibid; Editorial Board, "Florida restored voting rights to former felons. Now the GOP wants to thwart reform", *The Washington Post*, January 13, 2019, https://www.washingtonpost.com/opinions/florida-restored-voting-rights-to-former-felons-now-the-gop-wants-to-thwart-reform/2019/01/13/84e2dcdc-1520-11e9-803c-4ef28312c8b9_story.html; Abby Goodnough, "In a Break from the Past, Florida Will Let Felons Vote", *The New York Times*, April 6, 2007, https://www.nytimes.com/2007/04/06/us/06florida.html; and "Roadblocks to Restoring Rights", *Sarasota Herald-Tribune*, March 14, 2011, https://www.heraldtribune.com/news/20110314/roadblocks-to-restoring-rights/1.

85   Amy Gardner and Lori Rozsa, "Supreme Court deals blow to felons in Florida seeking to regain the right to vote", *The Washington Post*, July 16, 2020, https://www.washingtonpost.com/politics/supreme-court-deals-blow-to-felons-in-florida-seeking-to-regain-the-right-to-vote/2020/07/16/2ede827c-c5dd-11ea-a99f-3bbdffb1af38_story.html.

86   Ibid; Jason Breslow, "Florida Judge Rules Florida Law Restricting Voting Rights for Felons Unconstitutional", *National Public Radio*, May 24, 2020, https://www.npr.org/2020/05/24/861776313/federal-judge-rules-florida-law-restricting-voting-rights-for-felons-unconstitut.

87   Amy Gardner and Lori Rozsa, "Supreme Court deals blow to felons in Florida seeking to regain the right to vote", *The Washington Post*, July 16, 2020, https://www.washingtonpost.com/politics/supreme-court-deals-blow-to-felons-in-florida-seeking-to-regain-the-right-to-vote/2020/07/16/2ede827c-c5dd-11ea-a99f-3bbdffb1af38_story.html.

88   "Live Blog: Election Day 2016", *FORBES*, November 8, 2016, https://www.forbes.com/sites/kellyphillipserb/2016/11/08/live-blog-election-day-2016/#6d8b68322495.

89   Ibid.

90   Ibid.

91   Ibid.

92   Jonah Engel Bromwich, "Protests of Trump's Election Continue into Third Day", *The New York Times*, November 11, 2016, https://www.nytimes.com/2016/11/12/us/trump-election-protests.html.

93   Chris Howell, "What if more young people had voted in 2016?", *Towards Data Science*, January 10, 2020, https://towardsdatascience.com/what-if-more-young-people-had-voted-in-2016-7242f251f8e6.

94   "2000 Official Presidential General Election Results", *Federal Election Commission*, https://www.fec.gov/introduction-campaign-finance/election-and-voting-information/federal-elections-2000/president2000/.

95   Drew DeSilver, "U.S. trails most developed countries in voter turnout", *Pew Research Center*, May 21, 2018, https://www.pewresearch.org/fact-tank/2018/05/21/u-s-voter-turnout-trails-most-developed-countries/.

CHAPTER NINE

96   Jeffrey Goldberg, "Unthinkable, 50 Moments That Define and Improbable Presidency", *The Atlantic*, January 22, 2019, https://www.theatlantic.com/live/events/unthinkable-the-50-moments-that-define-the-trump/2019/.

97   Ibid.

98   Max Boot, "The Worst President Ever", *The Washington Post*, April, 5, 2020, https://www.washingtonpost.com/opinions/2020/04/05/worst-president-ever/

99   Michelle Mark, Kieran Corcoran and David Choi, "This timeline shows exactly how the Parkland shooting unfolded", *Business Insider*, February 14, 2019, https://www.businessinsider.com/timeline-shows-how-the-parkland-florida-school-shooting-unfolded-2018-2.

100   Chris Carson, "Celebrating Dr. Martin Luther King", *League of Women Voters*, January 15, 2017, https://www.lwv.org/blog/celebrating-dr-martin-luther-king-jrs-legacy.

101   "Martin Luther King Jr. Memorial Quotations", National Park Service, https://www.nps.gov/mlkm/learn/quotations.htm.

102   Casey Chapters, "How Have Florida Gun Laws Changed Since Parkland?", *WFSU Public Media*, February 14, 2019, https://news.wfsu.org/state-news/2019-02-14/how-have-floridas-gun-laws-changed-since-parkland.

103   "10 Fannie Lou Hamer Quotes to Celebrate Her 100th Birthday", *Because of Them We Can*, October 6, 2017, https://www.becauseofthemwecan.com/blogs/culture/10-fannie-lou-hamer-quotes-to-celebrate-her-100th-birthday.

104   The words are quoted exactly except for some minor spelling corrections on words that may have been unfamiliar to these youngsters when I used them verbally (i.e., my fast speaking tone led to some misspellings in their notes).

CHAPTER TEN

105   Ryan Bort, "This May Be the Most Bizarre 2018 Campaign Ad Yet", *Rolling Stone*, July 30, 2018, https://www.rollingstone.com/politics/politics-news/ron-desantis-trump-ad-704926/.

106 Siobhan Hughes, "Mitch McConnell Signals Limits on Race-Related Policy Changes", *The Wall Street Journal*, July 14, 2020, https://www.wsj.com/articles/mitch-mcconnell-signals-limits-on-race-related-policy-changes-11594733555.

107 Carol Hulse, "Moscow Mitch Tag Enrages McConnell and Squeezes GOP on Election Security", *The New York Times*, July 30, 2019, https://www.nytimes.com/2019/07/30/us/politics/moscow-mitch-mcconnell.html.

108 Khorri Atkinson, "Democrats won the House with the largest midterms margin of all time", *Axios*, November 27, 2018, https://www.axios.com/2018-midterm-elections-democrats-won-house-biggest-margin-a56a1049-8823-4667-8d81-2c67ef3f36f4.html.

109 Jonathan Allen and Alan Smith, "Gillum officially concedes Florida governor race, congratulates DeSantis on winning", *NBC News*, November 17, 2018, https://www.nbcnews.com/politics/elections/gillum-officially-concedes-florida-governor-race-congratulates-desantis-winning-n936786; Monivette Cordeiro, "Rick Scott restored the voting rights of twice as many white former felons as black felons", *Orlando Weekly*, October 31, 2018, https://www.orlandoweekly.com/Blogs/archives/2018/10/31/rick-scott-restored-the-voting-rights-of-twice-as-many-white-former-felons-as-black-felons.

110 Jonathan Allen and Alan Smith, "Gillum officially concedes Florida governor race, congratulates DeSantis on winning", *NBC News*, November 17, 2018, https://www.nbcnews.com/politics/elections/gillum-officially-concedes-florida-governor-race-congratulates-desantis-winning-n936786.

111 "Editorial: In the worst public health crisis in generations, DeSantis is a massive fail", *Naples Daily News*, July 17, 2020, https://www.naplesnews.com/story/opinion/2020/07/17/governor-ron-desantis-failing-public-health-crisis/5459005002/.

CHAPTER ELEVEN

112 "New Study Sheds Light on the 100 Million Americans Who Don't Vote, Their Political Views and What They Think About 2020", The John S. and James L. Knight Foundation, February 19, 2020, https://knightfoundation.org/press/releases/new-study-sheds-light-on-the-100-million-americans-who-dont-vote-their-political-views-and-what-they-think-about-2020/; Michael P. McDonald, "Voter Turnout National Turnout Rates, 1787-2018", *United States Election Project*, July 20, 2020, http://www.electproject.org/home/voter-turnout/voter-turnout-data.

113 Ibid.

114 Ibid.

115 Ibid.

116   "10 Fannie Lou Hamer Quotes to Celebrate Her 100th Birthday", *Because of Them We Can*, October 6, 2017, https://www.becauseofthemwecan.com/blogs/culture/10-fannie-lou-hamer-quotes-to-celebrate-her-100th-birthday.

117   Katherine Q. Seelye, "John Lewis, Towering Figure of Civil Rights Era, Dies at 80", *The New York Times*, July 17, 2020, https://www.nytimes.com/2020/07/17/us/john-lewis-dead.html.

118   Mary Irby-Jones, "Opinion: Mississippi flag vote is first of many needed changes in our state", *Hattiesburg American*, July 5, 2020, https://www.hattiesburgamerican.com/story/news/2020/07/05/opinion-mississippi-flag-vote-first-many-changes-needed-state/3278851001/.

119   Teri Weaver, "How they voted: NY lawmakers approve 10 police reform bills in 3 days", June 10, 2020, https://www.syracuse.com/crime/2020/06/how-they-voted-ny-lawmakers-approve-10-police-reform-bills-in-3-days.html.

120   Fred Kaplan, "Obtuse Engel", *SLATE*, June 24, 2020, https://slate.com/news-and-politics/2020/06/eliot-engel-jamaal-bowman-foreign-policy.html.

121   Ibid.

122   Kaleigh Rogers and Nathaniel Rakich, "Voter Registrations are Way, Way Down During the Pandemic", *FiveThirtyEight*, June 26, 2020, https://fivethirtyeight.com/features/voter-registrations-are-way-way-down-during-the-pandemic/.

123   Ibid.

124   Ibid.

125   Ibid.

126   Ibid.

127   "Automatic Voter Registration", *National Conference of State Legislatures*, April 14, 2020, https://www.ncsl.org/research/elections-and-campaigns/automatic-voter-registration.aspx.

128   "Automatic Voter Registration, a Summary", *Brennan Center for Justice*, July 10, 2019, https://www.brennancenter.org/our-work/research-reports/automatic-voter-registration-summary.

129   Ibid.

130   Zak Cheney-Rice, "Brian Kemp Seemed to Really Enjoy Suppressing Votes, Report Finds", *New York Magazine*, February 27, 2020, https://nymag.com/intelligencer/2020/02/brian-kemp-enjoyed-suppressing-votes.html.

131   The Editorial Board, "Voting Should be Easy. Why Isn't It", *New York Times*, October 18, 2018, https://www.nytimes.com/2018/10/18/opinion/registration-vote-midterms.html.

132   Kevin Morris, Myrna Perez, Jonathan Brater and Christopher Delazio, "Purges: A Growing Threat to the Right to Vote", *Brennan Center for Justice*, July 20, 2018,

https://www.brennancenter.org/our-work/research-reports/purges-growing-threat-right-vote.

133   Ibid.

134   Ibid.

135   Josh Gerstein, "Liberals recoil at SCOTUS' Wisconsin primary decision", *Politico*, April 7, 2020, https://www.politico.com/news/2020/04/07/liberals-recoil-at-su-preme-court-decision-on-wisconsin-primary-171347; Molly Ball, "What Went Wrong in the Wisconsin Election and What We Can Learn From It Before November", *Time*, April 9, 2020, https://time.com/5818773/wisconsin-coronavirus-elections/.

136   Molly Ball, "What Went Wrong in the Wisconsin Election and What We Can Learn From It Before November", *Time*, April 9, 2020, https://time.com/5818773/wisconsin-coronavirus-elections/.

137   Elise Viebeck, Amy Gardner, Dan Simmons and Jan M. Larson, "Long lines, anger and fear of infection: Wisconsin proceeds with elections under court order", *The Washington Post*, April 7, 2020, https://www.washingtonpost.com/politics/long-lines-form-in-milwaukee-as-wisconsin-proceeds-with-elections-under-court-order/2020/04/07/93727b34-78c7-11ea-b6ff-597f170df8f8_story.html.

138   David Wahlberg, "71 People who went to the polls on April 7 got COVID-19; tie to election uncertain", *Wisconsin State Journal*, May 16, 2020, https://madison.com/wsj/news/local/health-med-fit/71-people-who-went-to-the-polls-on-april-7-got-covid-19-tie-to/article_ef5ab183-8e29-579a-a52b-1de069c320c7.html.

139   Ibid.

140   Ella Nilsen and Li Zhou, "How Wisconsin's election disenfranchised voters", *VOX*, April 7, 2020, https://www.vox.com/2020/4/7/21212053/wisconsin-election-coronavirus-disenfranchised-voters.

141   Reid J. Epstein, "Upset Victory in Wisconsin Supreme Court Race Gives Democrats a Lift", *The New York Times*, April 13, 2020, https://www.nytimes.com/2020/04/13/us/politics/wisconsin-primary-results.html.

142   David Daley, "Georgia 's voting fiasco is a warning. The November election could be chaos.", *The Guardian*, June 11, 2020, https://www.theguardian.com/commentisfree/2020/jun/11/georgia-election-chaos-november.

143   Ibid.

144   Elura Nunos, "Conservative Majority of SCOTUS Grants Stay, Allows Alabama Voting Registration to Stay in Place During Pandemic", *LAW & CRIME*,   July 2, 2020, https://lawandcrime.com/supreme-court/conservative-majority-of-scotus-grants-stay-allows-alabama-voting-restrictions-to-stay-in-place-during-pandemic/.

145   Ibid.

146   The Editorial Board, "Voting Should be Easy. Why Isn't It", *New York Times*, October 18, 2018, https://www.nytimes.com/2018/10/18/opinion/registration-vote-midterms.html.

147   Ibid.

148   Ibid.

149   Ibid.

150   Aaron Blake, "Trump just comes out and says it: The GOP is hurt when it's easier to vote", *The Washington Post*, March 30, 2020, https://www.washingtonpost.com/politics/2020/03/30/trump-voting-republicans/.

151   "Debunking the Voter Fraud Myth", *Brennan Center for Justice*, January 31, 2017, https://www.brennancenter.org/our-work/research-reports/debunking-voter-fraud-myth; Max Feldman, "10 Voter Fraud Lies Debunked", *Brennan Center for Justice*, May 27, 2020, https://www.brennancenter.org/our-work/research-reports/10-voter-fraud-lies-debunked.

152   "Debunking the Voter Fraud Myth", *Brennan Center for Justice*, January 31, 2017, https://www.brennancenter.org/our-work/research-reports/debunking-voter-fraud-myth.

153   Elizabeth Landers, Eli Watkins and Kevin Liptak, "Trump dissolves voter fraud commission; adviser says it went 'off the rails'", *CNN*, January 4, 2018, https://www.cnn.com/2018/01/03/politics/presidential-election-commission/index.html.

154   Christopher Ingraham, "Universal vote-by-mail doesn't benefit any political party, study finds", *The Washington Post*, April 16, 2020, https://www.washingtonpost.com/business/2020/04/16/universal-vote-by-mail-doesnt-benefit-any-political-party-study-finds/.

155   Ben Christopher, "California, 2020 all-mail election explained", *CAL MATTERS*, June 25, 2020, https://calmatters.org/explainers/california-all-mail-election-explained-november-2020/.

156   Nathaniel Rakich, "Few States Are Prepared to Switch to Voting by Mail. That Could Make For a Messy Election", *FiveThirtyEight*, April 27, 2020, https://fivethirtyeight.com/features/few-states-are-prepared-to-switch-to-voting-by-mail-that-could-make-for-a-messy-election/.

157   Ibid.

158   Jane C. Timm, "States reject tens of thousands of mail in ballots in this year's primaries, setting off alarm bells for November", *NBC News*, July 18, 2020, https://www.nbcnews.com/politics/2020-election/states-reject-tens-thousands-mail-ballots-year-s-primaries-setting-n1233833.

159   Ibid.

160   Ibid.

161   Lori Robertson, "More False Mail-In Ballot Claims from Trump", May 27, 2020, https://www.factcheck.org/2020/05/more-false-mail-in-ballot-claims-from-trump/.

162   David M. Thompson et al., "Universal Vote-By-Mail Has No Impact on Partisan Turnout or Vote Share", *Democracy & Polarization Lab, Stanford University*, May 6, 2020.

163   Lori Robertson, "More False Mail-In Ballot Claims from Trump", May 27, 2020, https://www.factcheck.org/2020/05/more-false-mail-in-ballot-claims-from-trump/.

164   Holmes Lybrand and Tara Subramaniam, "Fact-checking Trump's recent claims that mail-in voting is rife with fraud", *CNN*, May 28, 2020, https://www.cnn.com/2020/07/30/politics/trump-delay-election-fact-check/index.html.

165   Richard L. Hasen, "Trump's bogus attacks on mail-in voting could hurt his supporters too", *The Washington Post*, May 20, 2020, https://www.washingtonpost.com/outlook/2020/05/20/trump-mail-vote-fraud/.

166   Donald K. Sherman, "Trump's new postmaster general could corrupt a key institution ahead of Election Day", *NBC News*, July 19, 2020, https://www.nbcnews.com/think/opinion/trump-s-2020-usps-appointment-could-corrupt-key-institution-ahead-ncna1234125.

167   Caitlin Oprysko, "House passes voting rights package aimed at restoring protections", *Politico*, December 6, 2019, https://www.politico.com/news/2019/12/06/house-passes-voting-rights-package-077112; League of Women Voters of Kentucky, "Mitch McConnell, let's end efforts to suppress the vote of black and poor people", *Courier Journal*, June 12, 2020, https://www.courier-journal.com/story/opinion/2020/06/12/voter-suppression-mcconnell-support-voting-rights-advancement-act/5337201002/.

168   "What is the For the People Act – also known as H.R.1?", *Common Cause*, January 4, 2019, https://www.commoncause.org/democracy-wire/what-is-the-for-the-people-act-also-known-as-h-r-1/.

169   Timothy E. Wirth and Tom Rogers, "How Trump Could Lose the Election – And Still Remain president/Opinion", *Newsweek*, July 3, 2020, https://www.newsweek.com/how-trump-could-lose-election-still-remain-president-opinion-1513975.

170   Ibid.

171   Ibid.

172   "10 Quotes from great minds on why you should vote", February 29, 2020, https://bigthink.com/politics-current-affairs/quotes-voting-thinkers.

173   "Fannie Lou Hamer Quotes and Sayings", www.inspiringquotes.us.